D0255610

THE CITIES OF
ANCIENT MEXICO

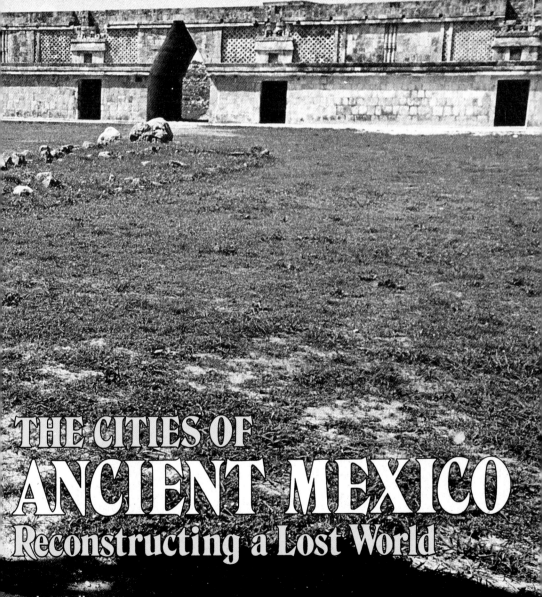

JEREMY A. SABLOFF

Special Photography by Macduff Everton

REVISED EDITION

THE CITIES OF
ANCIENT MEXICO
Reconstructing a Lost World

With 152 illustrations

COVER ILLUSTRATION: View to the north of System IV at Monte Alban. Photo Colin McEwan

TITLE PAGE: The "Nunnery," Uxmal. Photo Macduff Everton

First published in the United States of America in 1989 by Thames and Hudson Inc., 500 Fifth Avenue, New York, New York 10110

Revised edition 1997

Library of Congress Catalog Card Number 96-61016 ISBN 0-500-27929-2

Printed and bound in Hong Kong

For Paula Lynne Weinberg Sabloff

Contents

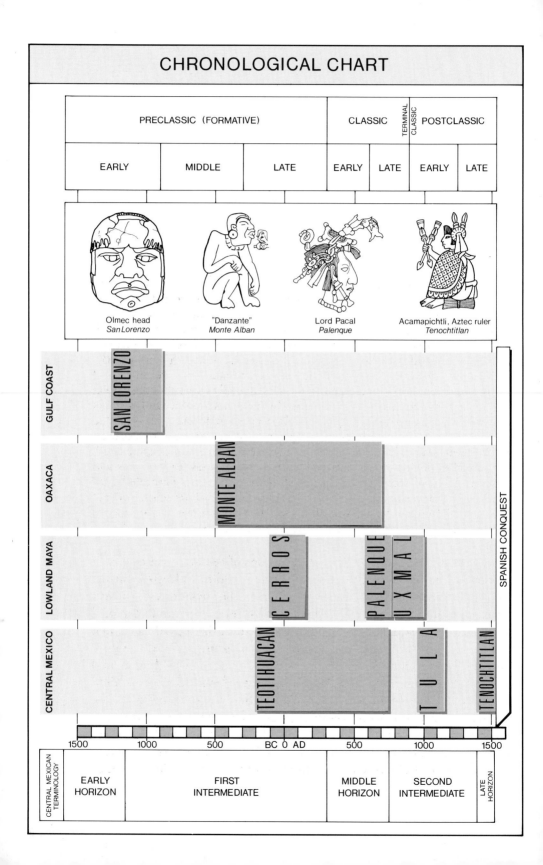

CHRONOLOGICAL CHART

| PRECLASSIC (FORMATIVE) | | | CLASSIC | | TERMINAL CLASSIC | POSTCLASSIC | |
| EARLY | MIDDLE | LATE | EARLY | LATE | | EARLY | LATE |

Olmec head *San Lorenzo*

"Danzante" *Monte Alban*

Lord Pacal *Palenque*

Acamapichtli, Aztec ruler *Tenochtitlan*

GULF COAST — SAN LORENZO

OAXACA — MONTE ALBAN

LOWLAND MAYA — CERROS · PALENQUE · UXMAL

CENTRAL MEXICO — TEOTIHUACAN · TULA · TENOCHTITLAN

SPANISH CONQUEST

1500   1000   500   BC 0 AD   500   1000   1500

| CENTRAL MEXICAN TERMINOLOGY | EARLY HORIZON | FIRST INTERMEDIATE | MIDDLE HORIZON | SECOND INTERMEDIATE | LATE HORIZON |

Introduction

Montezuma had two houses stocked with every sort of weapon; many of them were richly adorned with gold and precious stones. There were shields large and small, and a sort of broadsword, and two-handed swords set with flint blades that cut much better than our swords, and lances longer than ours, with five-foot blades consisting of many knives. Even when these are driven at a buckler or a shield they are not deflected. In fact they cut like razors, and the Indians can shave their heads with them. They had very good bows and arrows, and double and single-pointed javelins as well as their throwing-sticks and many slings and round stones shaped by hand, and another sort of shield that can be rolled up when they are not fighting, so that it does not get in the way, but which can be opened when they need it in battle and covers their bodies from head to foot. There was also a great deal of cotton armour which they used as devices and distinguishing marks, and they had casques and helmets made of wood and bone which were also highly decorated with feathers on the outside. They had other arms of different kinds which I will not mention through feat of prolixity, and workmen skilled in the manufacture of such things, and stewards who were in charge of these arms.[1]

Bernal Díaz del Castillo's vivid descriptions of the great Aztec city of Tenochtitlan, based on his experiences as a soldier in Cortés's army, are well known to those long fascinated by the mysteries of ancient Mexico. When he tells us: "The top of the *cue* [pyramid-temple] formed an open square on which stood something like a platform, and it was here that the great stones stood on which they placed the poor Indians for sacrifice. Here also was a massive image like a dragon, and other hideous figures, and a great deal of blood that had been spilled that day . . ."[2] we feel we can almost touch the "dragon" and smell the blood. The sixteenth-century descriptions of Tenochtitlan at the time of the Spanish Conquest, together with spectacular archaeological discoveries beneath modern-day Mexico City – now covering ancient Tenochtitlan – help us to picture life in that city nearly 500 years ago.

1 (*above*) Grim testimony of Aztec ritual: A sacrificial victim has his heart torn out in this sixteenth-century vignette of the shrines to Tlaloc and Huitzilopochtli – Aztec gods of water and war respectively – that crowned the Great Temple of Tenochtitlan.

2 (*right*) The Aztec capital Tenochtitlan as it appeared to the Spanish at the time of the Conquest.

But how can archaeologists conjure up pictures of other ancient cities when there are no historical descriptions? What would a site – say, the Maya city of Sayil that I studied between 1983 and 1988 – look like if we could step into a time-machine and see it as it was in its heyday?

This is exactly the kind of question that I get asked all the time – on the site itself, at lectures, or informally among friends. And it is a fair question, not to be ducked or avoided. It demands an effort. I might try to answer it like this:

It is mid-morning in the early summer of AD 810 (or, in the local calendar: the nineteenth *katun* of the ninth *baktun*). Sayil hums with activity. It and the other cities of the Puuc region are reaching the height of their prosperity and power.

The main city center of Sayil covers an area of more than 3 square kilometers, although fields cultivated with crops such as maize can be seen in the surrounding valleys and on the hillsides, and houses are scattered as far as the eye can see. Within the city, large stone buildings up to three stories high jut up between smaller structures, some of stone, others of wood and thatch.

In the southern part of the city stands a huge rectangular, two-storied building that houses the city's administration, full of bureaucrats in their offices and petitioners hurrying from one to another. To the north of this building is the paved market, its empty stands awaiting the crowds that will flock there the next day. Just to the east workmen are finishing repairs to the great ball court.

The Maya ball game, unlike our modern sporting events, is a combination of religious ritual and political ceremony. It is also used to resolve disputes. Only a limited elite – such as dignitaries from the nearby cities of Uxmal, Kabah, and Labna – can watch it. Since the southern Classic Maya centers, Tikal and Copan among them, faded from history over a century before, it is the cities in the Puuc region which, together with Chichen Itza to the northeast, are among the dominant powers in the lowland Maya realm. Relations between the other Puuc cities and Sayil are close, and the rites celebrated at the beginning of summer are a time for confirming their solidarity. The ball game is one of the highlights.

The elite who work in the administrative center live just to the west of it. Their houses are large, constructed of stone, and beautifully decorated; they are built on platforms, either singly or in groups nestling around small plazas.

The ruling family of Sayil lives in the Great Palace about a kilometer north of the administrative center. It is an imposing building, three stories high and containing nearly 100 rooms, dwarfing everything around it. It provides accommodation not only for the ruling family with all its extensions, but also for more distant relations, retainers and servants. If we go inside we find a few grand public rooms with colonnaded entries, but the private quarters are relatively narrow, often leading off each other without exterior windows. As our eyes become accustomed to the gloom, paintings can be seen on some of the walls; most, however, are covered only with white plaster. Doorways may have curtains hanging from wooden poles, while some floors are covered by woven mats. The ceilings have high corbeled arches and wooden beams.

A striking feature of Sayil is the elaborate provision made for conserving water. Private houses, and even the large palaces, have big underground cisterns sunk into the platforms beneath them. With no rivers and few permanent springs in the Puuc region, virtually all the water has to be collected from rainfall. Although there is a long and heavy rainy season in the second half of the year, the months between January and May are dry. At the time of our visit, water levels are low. Not even the ruling family can afford to be extravagant.

Between the administrative center and the Great Palace runs a huge causeway. On major state occasions the ruler, bedecked in animal skins, jewelry of finely carved green jade and an elaborate feather headdress, parades along it, stopping at the shrines and other religious sites. With his large retinue, he is a dazzling figure to the cheering crowds that have turned out to greet him.

Just before the causeway reaches the ball court at its southern end, it passes a platform displaying sculpted and painted monuments and altars. This is the shrine to the ruler's ancestors, who are commemorated in pictures and inscriptions. Here the ruler pauses to honor his forebears and the gods by shedding his own blood. With a sharp obsidian knife he pierces his ear lobes and tongue. The blood drips into a decorated bowl held by an attendant to prevent his beautiful costume being spattered. The bowl is then handed to a priest who offers the blood to the gods. The procession passes on. . . .

That, or something like it, would be one way of answering questions that begin: "If you could step into a time-machine . . ." And I must admit that such questions are a challenge to any archaeologist, more at ease perhaps with studying the minutiae of an ancient site's stratigraphy than with having to reconstruct the life of its inhabitants. Through such innocent inquiries the scholar is forced to confront further major issues such as: "But what is your evidence? How are you able to make such statements?" The kind of historical vignette that I briefly sketched above – what one colleague has dubbed a "just-so story" – is useful, but it demands more justification. I have therefore organized this book on the following lines.

3 The Mexican ball game as represented in a sixteenth-century codex. The skulls are an indication that the game may have been played "to the death," the defeated captain losing not just the match but his life as well. Compare ill. 29.

In the first Part I pose questions of the form: "What might I see if I glimpsed a particular city through the eyes of one of its inhabitants *x* number of years ago?" To provide an answer I put together a series of vignettes relating the currently visible remains to what we know of their past from all sources. The sites themselves are chosen and arranged in such a way as to illustrate the origins and continuity of ancient Mexican civilization from the Olmecs to the Aztecs, a period of some 3,000 years. I take the opportunity in Part II to examine a variety of questions about cultural diffusion and possible influences from outside, and to comment on the provocative ideas of various authors from Heyerdahl to Von Däniken.

4 The Great Palace, a three-story structure with nearly 100 rooms, at the Maya city of Sayil.

Part III discusses *how* archaeologists attempt to attach meaning to the remains they survey and excavate. This section introduces the reader to archaeological methods in general, the problems with analogies, and the means by which they may be strengthened. I then turn to a discussion of how archaeologists interested in ancient Mexican civilization in particular have used analogies in their area. Over the years, these scholars have noted numerous cultural continuities from ancient through historic to modern times. One of the most obvious of these is language. For instance, Nahua in Central Mexico, Zapotec and Mixtec in Oaxaca, and a variety of Mayan languages in the

Maya Lowlands and Highlands were spoken in Precolumbian times and are still widely used today. Continuity may also be seen in methods of food preparation and in kinship practices, although there is much debate on the severity of the changes wrought by the Spanish Conquest. Lastly, I examine some of the inferences made in the vignettes and indicate which of these inferences are based on secure analogies, which are purely speculative, and which lie somewhere in between.

PART I

What were the cities like?

CHAPTER ONE

Hunters, Villagers, and City-Dwellers

The beginning of Mexican civilization dates to about 1200 BC with the rise of many complex societies or "chiefdoms," such as the Olmecs, Zapotecs, and Zoques, among many others. Although the Olmecs have traditionally been viewed as the first of a series of civilizations that culminated in the Aztecs just prior to the Spanish Conquest nearly three millennia later, some archaeologists have argued that it is preferable to consider the cultural developments from 1500 BC to the sixteenth century AD as one complex system with various flowerings through time and space. Such a view is more than mere semantic fiddling; it indicates how impressed scholars are with the interconnectedness of ancient Mexican cultures.

Anthropologists maintain that much of modern-day Mexico and neighboring areas, including Guatemala, Belize, and parts of Honduras and El Salvador, formed a *culture area* that is usually labeled "Mesoamerica." The Mesoamerican culture area has traditionally been defined as the extent of the distribution of a complex of traits, including early cultivation of maize and the use of calendars, that are seen as setting the area apart from its neighbors to the north and south. This area had such a high level of interaction, including trade and movement of peoples, that changes or innovation in one part would affect all the other parts. While we will concentrate our attention on the greater part of this system that lies within the borders of modern-day Mexico, we will also examine its southern lowland extension that flourished in the neighboring countries of Central America.

By 1000 BC, it is clear that many regions in ancient Mexico had developed close contacts. Most of these contacts had to do with the exchange of raw materials, such as obsidian or magnetite, as well as marine shells and stingray spines. Finished craft products, such as finely carved jade, began to be exchanged a few centuries later. It is

5,6 **A world without wheeled vehicles** Wheeled "toys" such as this one from Veracruz (*below*), show that the ancient Mexicans knew the principle of the wheel well enough. But without beasts of burden to provide traction, wheeled vehicles were never developed in the New World, and traders relied on people like these porters (*above*) to transport goods.

likely that non-material ideas and beliefs were exchanged along the same routes. Over the next 2,500 years, these contacts and exchanges grew stronger and increasingly regularized as the system became more complex and centralized.

Without cows, horses, donkeys, or oxen available to be domesticated, traction animals, pack animals, and general beasts of burden were completely absent in ancient Mexico. The relative lack of animal domestication in the area (with some minor exceptions such as the turkey), lent a particular character to the exchange of goods, which differed from the pattern in other parts of the world like the ancient Near East where animals helped move bulk commodities over long distances. Technology was also much more limited in Mexico than in the Near East. For some as yet unexplained reason, metallurgy did not become important in Mexico until relatively late in the sequence, and even then metal was used principally for ceremonial items rather than for tools. Perhaps because of the absence of traction animals, wheeled vehicles were lacking in ancient Mexico, although the concept of the wheel was known (as witnessed by the small wheeled toys found in sites in the Gulf Coast Lowlands). Human labor was thus critical in the movement of materials in Mexico; raw materials and finished goods had to be carried mainly on the backs of porters. Warfare, too, had a different flavor, since there were no chariots or cavalry. The army consisted only of infantry, and battles seem to have been fought as clashes of individual soldiers, not coordinated groups. Despite these technological limitations, the peoples of ancient Mexico were able to weave an exceedingly complex web of economic, social, political, and religious interconnections.

The geographic setting

Cultural contacts in ancient Mesoamerica are particularly fascinating because of the extremely diverse environments that were linked in Precolumbian times. These ranged from semi-arid mountainous basins to tropical rainforest lowlands. Coastal areas, river valleys, and lake shores all presented suitable sites for occupation. By 1000 BC all those zones were occupied, and materials were being exchanged from one to another. The environmental variety and the differential availability of both mineral and plant resources which this presented, led to the regular movement of goods and was one of the main factors contributing to the growth of complex societies in the area.

The Mexican environment

Ancient Mexican civilization developed in a wide variety of environments with differing natural potentials, from jungle Lowlands to Highland valleys.

7 (*above*) The Valley of Oaxaca, showing modern agricultural fields.

8 (*left*) Burning an agricultural field in the tropical rain forest of the Southern Maya Lowlands, near Uaxactun, prior to planting.

9 (*right*) Lake Texcoco in the Basin of Mexico. Much of this lake has been drained since the Spanish Conquest.

Two highland and two lowland regions were the principal foci of complex developments. These were the tropical Lowlands of the Gulf Coast (the modern Mexican states of Veracruz and Tabasco); the Lowlands of the Yucatan peninsula; the highland Valley of Oaxaca; and the Highlands of Central Mexico (especially the Basin of Mexico and surrounding area).

The two lowland regions are quite diverse and include zones of tropical rainforest, or jungle, with dense vegetation and high rainfall; numerous rivers in the Gulf Coast that flow down from the highlands to the Gulf of Mexico; low scrub forests in Northern Yucatan with very distinct dry and rainy seasons; and the small, volcanic Tuxtla Mountains of Veracruz. The rugged highland regions are characterized by mountain chains, including volcanoes surrounding the Basin of Mexico that reach heights of over 5,000 meters. In Precolumbian times, the Basin of Mexico, situated at the junction of the two spines of the Sierra Madre mountain chains, contained a series of lakes that have been subsequently drained and covered to a large extent by the sprawling features of the gigantic urban zone of modern-day Mexico City. The Valley of Oaxaca, to the south, is a large plateau lying in the continuation of the Sierra Madre mountain chain.

Ancient Mexicans made full use of the distinct opportunities for exploitation that the lowland and highland environments offered. Upland riverine valleys contained choice locations for intensive irrigation agriculture, and the mountain zones had abundant minerals for mining. The Lowlands presented different opportunities for the ancient agriculturalists, particularly in the form of extensive swidden or slash-and-burn farming (a shifting form of cultivation where a field may be used for two or three years and then left fallow for eight or ten), although, as archaeologists have recently discovered, some forms of intensive agriculture were practiced there, too. In addition, important "cash" crops such as cacao and cotton could be grown in the Lowlands. Many of the minerals available in the Highlands were lacking here, however, with the exception of salt. We shall reexamine these specific environmental features in our discussion below.

Settled village life: Foundation for urban civilization

The antiquity of human occupation in the New World is much shorter than in the Old. Scholars argue heatedly about the precise dates, but strong evidence for a human presence in ancient Mexico does not go back much further than about 12,000 years ago. In fact, in few places in the Americas is there firm proof of human settlement before this date and some archaeologists have argued that it represents the time of the first peopling of the New World. The original colonists – whether 12,000, 15,000 or 20,000 years ago – crossed from Asia via a land bridge that connected Alaska to Siberia at the end of the last Ice Age. They quickly radiated throughout North, Central, and South America. Evidence for early occupation of ancient Mexico includes finds of spear points, both in isolation and in association with now-extinct mammals.

With the end of the Ice Age some 10,000 years ago, human occupants of the New World slowly adapted to a changing environment. Many of the big game animals, on whom human hunters had preyed, died out, leading to a shift of emphasis in the diet toward plant foods. Archaeological research in such places as the Tehuacan Valley in the southern Puebla Highlands and the Valley of Oaxaca has shown that for many millennia, from the end of the last glacial period to the beginning of Formative or Preclassic times (after 2000 BC), people exploited a number of wild plants. These ancient hunters and gatherers practiced a nomadic lifeway, moving their camps seasonally as the vegetation changed. Their experiments over thousands of years, particularly with the wild ancestors of maize (corn), ultimately provided them with sufficient surpluses for storage and use throughout the year and led to the development of agriculture. This availability of foodstuffs in one place through the different seasons in turn made it possible to establish semi-permanent or permanent settlements. Villages gradually developed and were present in many parts of ancient Mexico between about 2000 and 1000 BC.

Before the close of the second millennium BC certain regions began to display a growing cultural complexity. Moreover, these regions seem to have regularly interacted with each other. Non-domestic, "public" architecture appeared, and structures and artifacts that seem to have had religious significance are found. It is in fact not at all easy to demonstrate religious significance, but for want of a better term archaeologists tend to apply the label "ceremonial" in such circumstances, whether or not a ritual function can be proved. This increasing complexity has been found in the Lowlands of the Gulf Coast, the piedmont and coast of Chiapas, the Basin of Mexico, and the Valley of Oaxaca. It is in the latter region that the first true city of ancient Mexico emerged.

What is a city?

Scholars rarely agree about the exact definition of a city: are streets and public buildings essential components? Should there be evidence of a ruling class and writing systems? Are size, number of people, or density of people the main criteria? One thing is certain: when studying the cities of ancient Mexico preconceptions based on modern cities must be cast aside.

10 (*left*) London, a 2,000-year-old city. The medieval pattern of narrow, winding streets, the importance of religious buildings (churches), and the city's major role as a port are all displayed in this early-nineteenth-century view.

11 (*below*) An ancient Maya city: a reconstruction of Copan in the eighth century AD. The layout bears little resemblance to the modern city grid plan.

12 (*right*) New York by night. The illuminated skyscrapers and wide streets designed for vehicles are far removed from ancient Mexico's unlit cities.

The nature of ancient cities

We are so familiar with modern cities that it is difficult to imagine what their pre-industrial counterparts were like. Standing amidst the ruins of the great urban centers of ancient Mexico, it takes a strong act of will not to imagine them in terms of the cities we know. It is difficult, for instance, to visualize a city that is not lit up at night. But without electric power or gaslights, the cities of ancient Mexico had neither street lights, nor are there any indications that they were regularly lit by torches or other means.

One common preconception is that cities are laid out to aid the flow of traffic, whether it be cars or horse-drawn carriages. But with no automobiles, beasts of burden, or wheeled vehicles of any kind, the layout of ancient Mexican cities was not controlled by this factor. Instead, the streets and raised causeways of the cities of Precolumbian Mexico were few in number and of ritual importance. City planning tended to emphasize access (or lack thereof) to special places; the importance of local topographic features; or various ideological conceptions, such as particular astronomical orientations of buildings or whole centers – all quite different from concepts behind modern city development.

It is crucial for scholars to be aware of modern preconceptions about the nature of cities. Although impossible to eliminate, at least by bringing them to a conscious level it becomes easier to see and interpret various classes of archaeological data that might otherwise be ignored, or whose meaning might be falsely assumed. A wall around a city, for example, does not necessarily have a defensive function, especially if the ancient peoples' practice of warfare was significantly different from that of the Western world. Perhaps it had a political function, to demarcate territory; or a social one, to separate different groups. Walls might have been used to keep people, or animals, in, rather than to keep others out. As new information is uncovered through field research and historic studies, archaeologists are in a stronger position than ever before to characterize the major features of some of the best known urban centers.

Just what do we mean by "urban center" or "city"? Definition of these terms has been the subject of significant controversy in the scholarly literature. Much of the contention is over the inclusion or exclusion of particular traits that are deemed necessary markers of urbanization. Perhaps the most famous "trait list" is that of the archaeologist V. Gordon Childe. In his article, "The Urban Revolution," Childe listed ten criteria for the city, including size, the production of a variety of goods, the presence of a ruling class, and long distance trade.

Arguments over Childe's or other scholars' criteria have arisen either because of the difficulties in recognizing certain items in the archaeological record (such as standing armies), or else because of regional biases, such as the requirement of Near Eastern scholars that written records should be a necessary component of cities. But if one insists on including writing, for example, then Teotihuacan, a site with more than 120,000 inhabitants by AD 500 – and one of the largest places in the world at that time – cannot be considered a city because it shows slim evidence of writing. As Lewis Mumford has stated in *The City in History*, "No single definition will apply to all its manifestations and no single description will cover all its transformations."[3]

In recent years, many scholars have offered new definitions of cities that emphasize the relatedness of a series of trends or processes which they exhibit, in order to avoid some of the objections that the trait-list definitions generated. The archaeologist Charles Redman, for instance, has pointed out: "The most important quality defining a city is its complexity and form of integration. Cities are made up not simply of large populations but of large *diverse* populations that account for the economic and organizational diversity and interdependence that distinguishes a city from simpler settlement forms." He goes on to state:

"Most cities have the following characteristics:
1   A large and dense population
2   Complexity and interdependence
3   Formal and impersonal organization
4   Many nonagricultural activities
5   A diversity of central services both for its inhabitants and for the smaller communities in the surrounding area."[4]

We can simplify Redman's useful definition even further and follow the demographer Kingsley Davis's elegantly simple definition of the "city:" "a large settlement – a concentration of many people located close together for residential and protective purposes."[5] As a rule of thumb, some scholars have used the figure of about 5,000 people as a minimal gloss for "large."

The first cities of ancient Mexico began to emerge in the Valley of Oaxaca and the Valley of Mexico by the middle of the first millennium BC. These urban centers did not suddenly appear; their roots can be traced back through many centuries in both areas, as well as throughout Mesoamerica as a whole.

CHAPTER TWO

San Lorenzo and the Olmecs: Laying the Foundations for Mexican Civilization

San Lorenzo was one of the most important Gulf Coast Olmec centers, along with La Venta and Tres Zapotes, and is certainly the best-known site in terms of archaeological knowledge.

TIME: Dawn, early summer, about 1000 BC

PLACE: San Lorenzo, near the Coatzacoalcos River, Gulf Coast of Mexico

CIVILIZATION: Olmec

In the cold, wet hour just before dawn a weaver and her family awake. Although the tropical sun will push the temperature quite high by the afternoon, the early morning is chilly and damp. The members of the family quickly dress and eat a simple meal of corn gruel as the sky begins to lighten. The weaver[6] is anxious; she knows it will be a long, hard day, and that there will be no respite for several weeks.

The weaver devotes her days to making clothes, while her husband tills the family fields. She spins thread from cotton grown by the family and sews garments, such as cloaks and loincloths, with bone needles. From local plants she extracts dyes which she uses to color the threads and decorate the garments. Her most lucrative commissions are for the elite families in the ceremonial center on the great hill a little way upriver. In return for finished clothing she receives additional food, or exotic valuables such as the sharp obsidian blades that make cutting so much easier.

The woman and her family live in a thatch-roofed house that forms part of a hamlet with a population of nearly a dozen families, many of them related. The weaver herself has no close relatives of an older generation as both her husband's parents and her own are already dead. The hamlet is just one of many linked to the great ceremonial center, although a few, like the small village immediately upriver, are larger and more important.

Just the day before, a raft holding a huge carved stone head had been floated up to the landing at the foot of the hill crowned by the ceremonial center. Today, her husband and many of the other adult males in the surrounding communities have been called out by the chief to help pull the heavy basalt monument up the steep slope to the top of the hill. This important chore will take many days. The problem for the family is that their fields cannot be left untended for that length of time. So the weaver will have to look after them herself as well as try to complete an important commission for the chief's son, who wants an elaborately woven cloak for the ceremony dedicating the great stone head.

With everything organized for the day, the weaver sets off on a well-worn dirt path that leads from the river to the fields, while her husband heads for the riverbank. The youngest children go with him, already excited by the festival atmosphere that surrounds the effort to drag the huge monument from the river to the hilltop. Such irregular occasions bring together people from all the nearby communities, and they become great social events for those not directly involved in the hard labor. The weaver's family and many of the neighbors will paddle their small dugout canoes upriver to where the stone head has been brought.

The family works fields in the uplands. The highly productive lands by the river, flooded with rich new alluvium each year, are controlled almost exclusively by wealthy families from the ceremonial center. The upland fields are fairly productive but must be left fallow for a number of years after only a few years of cultivation.

The weaver walks for some time along the narrow trail through a high forest dominated by ceiba trees that have grown up over the years on uncultivated land, near plots currently being used, and through fields just recently let fallow. She finally reaches a familiar landmark and cuts off the main trail to her fields. The maize planted a couple of months earlier is growing well and should provide a good harvest, but the ever-present weeds pose a constant threat. The clearing work is slow and laborious: some weeds can be pulled out by the roots but others need to be cut with a stone axe. Soon after noon, the heat has become so intense that the weaver seeks the shade of a nearby tree. She quenches her thirst from a gourd full of water and eats a lunch of dried fish and tortillas.

By the time she arrives home, her eldest daughter is at work crushing kernels of corn on a metate, or grinding stone, in preparation for the evening meal. The resulting corn flour will be used as dough and mixed and cooked with another vegetable. They eat fresh fish when they can, caught in the river shallows or in isolated oxbow lakes. On rare occasions they enjoy the luxury of turtle meat.

Late in the afternoon the weaver's husband returns with their small children. They describe the immense effort required to haul the giant head from the raft onto the river bank. Great care had had to be taken not to damage the sculpture since the carving was already complete. Hundreds of men had had to use not just brute force but finesse as well in moving the head, under the direction of skilled leaders. Tomorrow the slow work of dragging the head along the specially prepared road to the foot of a sloping earthen ramp will begin. After that, the monolith will somehow be maneuvered up the ramp, to the summit of the hill.

Meanwhile the carved face is still enveloped in a protective covering of cotton padding. A portrait of the current chief, it has been carved by several well-known sculptors near the source of the basalt stone a few days' journey up into the mountains. The face will not be revealed until the dedication ceremony in several weeks, when the entire community, as well as the inhabitants of all the surrounding villages, will crowd into the great open plaza in the hilltop center.

The foundations of civilization: The Olmecs

In contrast to the slow growth of settled village life in ancient Mexico, many of the attributes of complex society appeared quite suddenly. The first cities of ancient Mexico – Monte Alban and then Teotihuacan – came into existence about 1,000 years after the rapid and widespread appearance of fully settled villages (in the mid-second millennium BC). The foundations for the rise of these cities were most *visibly* built by the Olmecs, although earlier conceptions of the Olmecs as the "mother culture" of Mexican civilization are now seen as being considerably exaggerated and oversimplified. In fact, many scholars now see the development of the Olmecs as just one among the many early Mexican developments towards complex civilization.

Much of our knowledge of Olmec civilization is based on research at only two principal sites, San Lorenzo and La Venta in the Gulf Coast Lowlands; with less than 1,000 residents each, these really were no more than small towns or large villages. The fieldwork of the

archaeologist Michael D. Coe and his associates at San Lorenzo has been instrumental in shaping our understanding of this crucially important, but little known, civilization. Coe found that the site was first occupied soon after 1500 BC. Within a hundred years or so, the first indications of the beginning of public works and architecture appeared, including the artificial buildup of the plateau upon which the site is situated, and the construction of a platform approximately 2 meters in height. Such a development is not unique to San Lorenzo but probably reflects a widespread trend in ancient Mexico as once-small villages grew in size, and structures for the use of the community at large were constructed by the new labor pool now available to the community. The organization of this labor, by whom and how, remains the subject of much debate. New research at the site may clarify such questions.

Over the next few centuries, the major cultural features by which the Olmecs are recognized, particularly in art style and artifacts, appear in the archaeological record. By 1150 BC, the Olmec style, with its

13,14 A mother teaching her daughter how to spin (*left*) and weave (*below left*), from a sixteenth-century codex. We can infer that weaving was present from the earliest days of civilization in ancient Mexico.

15 (*right*) A colossal Olmec head of basalt, found at San Lorenzo.

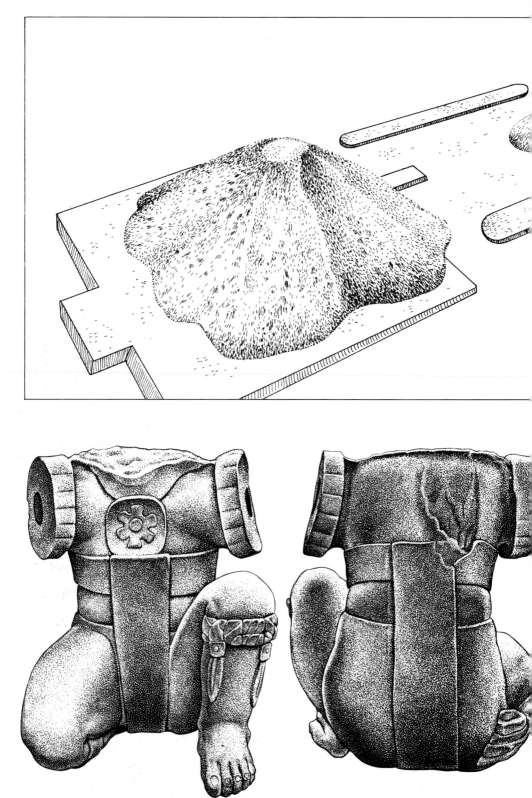

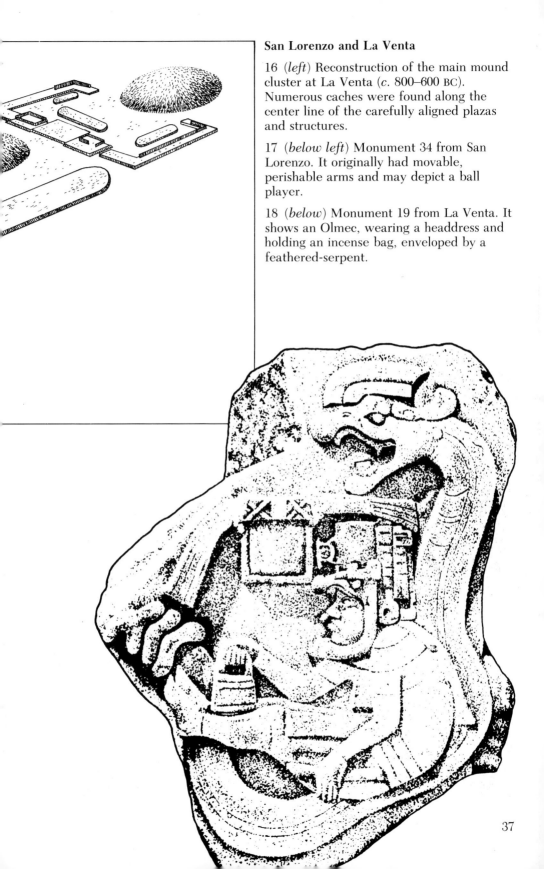

San Lorenzo and La Venta

16 (*left*) Reconstruction of the main mound cluster at La Venta (*c.* 800–600 BC). Numerous caches were found along the center line of the carefully aligned plazas and structures.

17 (*below left*) Monument 34 from San Lorenzo. It originally had movable, perishable arms and may depict a ball player.

18 (*below*) Monument 19 from La Venta. It shows an Olmec, wearing a headdress and holding an incense bag, enveloped by a feathered-serpent.

Olmec were-jaguars and baby-faced figurines

19,20,21 (*right*) Ceremonial axes: a greenstone axe (*near right*) from the Gulf of Mexico shows a typical Olmec "were-jaguar" figure with flaming eyebrows and a cleft forehead. Another carving (*center right*) represents a child-jaguar deity associated with rain. The so-called Kunz Axe (*far right*), made of greenstone, displays a were-jaguar clasping a miniature axe in its hands.

22 (*below*) Greenstone figure from Las Limas of an Olmec holding an infant deity, interpreted by some scholars as a rain deity.

23 (*below center*) A clay figurine from La Venta with baby-like facial features.

24 (*below right*) Offering 4 from La Venta. A lone granite figure faces a number of figures made from precious greenstone. The offering was deliberately buried with the sculptures arranged in this mysterious way.

25 Relief 1 from Chalcatzingo, a site that had contacts with the later Gulf Coast Olmecs. The carving has been interpreted by scholars such as Mary Miller and David Grove as an Olmec ruler seated on a throne within a cave mouth, in a schematic landscape where maize flourishes.

distinctive iconography that features the striking were-jaguar – a creature combining both human and feline aspects – can be found at San Lorenzo. Moreover, huge heads made from basalt stone are also found there, as well as at other large Olmec sites. These impressive heads weighed many tons each (sometimes over 20 tons), and appear to be portraits – possibly monuments to individual rulers. In addition, a wide variety of distinctive stone artifacts, ceramics, and sculptures made by the Olmecs are found in significant quantities. Some building was also being undertaken, as evidenced by the leveling-off of the huge platform and plaza upon which San Lorenzo sits, as well as by long-distance trade and the procurement of exotic materials. Magnetite and obsidian were imported into the Gulf Coast Lowlands, while the basalt for the great stone heads had to be transported, presumably by wooden rafts where possible, long distances (sometimes more than 100 kilometers) from their sources in the Tuxtla Mountains.

The need for new resources brought the Olmecs into contact with widespread groups of peoples, particularly those in the neighboring highlands. For example, the strategically located center of Chalcatzingo traded with them, as did sites from the Valley of Mexico, Oaxaca, and the southern frontier of Mesoamerica. It seems clear that the exchange of goods and ideas that resulted from these contacts helped lead to the establishment of the Mexican civilization that flourished for more than 2,500 years. Some scholars have also argued that the demand by the Olmecs for both raw materials and finished products would have stimulated the development of groups in the nearby highland zones, particularly ones that controlled natural resources or were situated astride potential trade routes. However, recent research in Oaxaca by Joyce Marcus and Kent Flannery indicates that sites like San Jose Mogote, although trading with the Gulf Coast Lowlands and elsewhere, had a long history of independent development, as did other precocious sites in the highlands of Chiapas.

Why do we find these early intensifications of political and artistic complexity in the Gulf Coast Lowlands? Michael Coe, among others, has suggested that the rich agricultural potential of the tropical environment and productive zones surrounding the large rivers (that flowed through the area northward from the Highlands to the Gulf of Mexico) could be exploited relatively easily without the heavy investments of labor that were necessary in the semi-arid Highlands. The power that control of these rich lands would have offered to particular family groups or individuals might well have been symbol-ized and solidified by, what were for the time, relatively large-scale building and sculptural projects. The need to import various raw materials has also been cited as an important stimulus for development in the Gulf Coast zone.

The heyday of the Olmecs lasted only a few centuries. They soon bowed to competition from the Highlands and were eclipsed by other contemporaneous groups, especially from Oaxaca. The Highlands, building on a base of direct control of raw materials, long histories of local development, and the potential for intensive agriculture, soon outstripped their lowland trading partners in economic and political development. The flexing of this new power, probably both by raiding and in the manipulation of trade, may have sounded the death knell for Olmec prosperity around 600 BC, but this date is not at all certain.

CHAPTER THREE

Monte Alban:
Sacred City of the Zapotecs

Several hundred years later, and a few hundred kilometers to the southwest, the inhabitants of the Valley of Oaxaca were beginning to see the material results of many centuries of continued development. They had been in contact with the Olmecs during the latter's florescence and their demographic, political, and economic strength had grown concomitantly. Moreover, Oaxacan control of regional trade became stronger through time and their influence began to spread beyond the immediate environs of the Valley. Building on this growing power base, an elite group founded the centrally located site of Monte Alban at about 500 BC. Over the next five centuries this center grew in size and importance, and it rapidly achieved urban proportions. As the largest site in the Valley of Oaxaca, it extended its military and economic influence well beyond the boundaries of the Valley.

TIME: About AD 1

PLACE: Monte Alban, Valley of Oaxaca, Southwest Mexico

CIVILIZATION: Zapotec

The astronomer woke with a start, fearing he had overslept, and peered out of his doorway. With great relief he saw it was still dark. He dressed hurriedly in the damp air of the late spring morning, and stepped outside. Quickly visiting several other houses, he woke up the occupants.

A few minutes later, a small group of men and women were walking up a steep path from the terraces on which their homes were built, heading for the large plaza on the hill above. This plaza formed the core of the growing city of Monte Alban, but in the early hours of the morning it was almost deserted.

The astronomer and his colleagues mounted the steps of a strangely shaped, arrow-like, building in the middle of the plaza. If their calendrical calculations were correct – and they and their assistants had spent many hours carefully checking them – today the sun would not produce any shadows when it reached its peak in the sky. After this great event (which happened twice a year), a major festival would commence with all kinds of associated ceremonies, including a ball game and the sacrificing of foreign soldiers captured in a recent military campaign. The whole city was waiting for the pronouncement that the great day had arrived.

As dawn approached, the astronomer stood at the top of the platform, facing directly down the stairs; this positioning was critical for his calculations. He lifted his eyes to the horizon, as one of his assistants handed him two sacred sticks. He raised the sticks, tied by a piece of leather into the shape of a cross, put them to his eye-level and sighted just above the horizon through the top notch. He knew from long experience that, apart from a ritual purpose, the sticks' main function was to help him focus on the correct place on the horizon. He waited with growing impatience. Suddenly, there, visible between the crossed sticks, was the bright star glimmering just above the horizon. Now they could be certain that the gods would favor them with the sun that cast no shadows at midday. The astronomer quickly sent his assistant to inform the high priest of the great event and accompany him here to the observatory. The old religious leader soon arrived to confirm that the star had appeared and that this was to be the day of no shadow. With invocations to the gods he inaugurated the day-long celebrations in Monte Alban.

The astronomer now returned to his house and changed into his robe, decorated cloak, and feather headdress, which he was required by tradition to wear for the forthcoming ceremonies. He saw with irritation that one of the garments had trailed in the tamped earth floor of the house, and was now scarcely fit to be worn.

He hurried back to the great plaza. The sun was already well up in the sky, and hundreds of people were milling about. At the memorial monument that glorified Monte Alban's great triumphs in battle, preparations were underway for the opening ceremonies of the festival. Along the sides of the building, rows of carved stone panels depicted the glyphs of towns that the city had conquered. Here, today, several recently captured enemies would be sacrificed to the gods.

The crowds gathered, and the prisoners were prepared for the rituals. The ruler signaled for the ceremony to begin. The drums began to beat and the captured enemy soldiers, dressed in simple white loincloths, were led forward to the altar in front of the stairway. The priest, who had positioned himself at the foot of the stair, leaned over the first captive who was stretched on his back over the altar, his arms and legs held by four acolytes. The priest readied his knife. The large black obsidian blade flashed in the sun as it plunged into the captive's chest. His heart was ripped out and offered to the gods with a fervent prayer for a bountiful, wet, growing season. A roar went up from the crowd. The festival had begun.

26 Structure J at Monte Alban, viewed from the south. Its principal function seems to have been as a monument to military conquests. It also had a significant astronomical orientation.

The Valley of Oaxaca

If, as some scholars have argued, the foundations for the rise of cities were laid by the Olmecs, then the actual construction must be credited to the highland peoples of Oaxaca, Morelos, and the Valley of Mexico. These peoples had contacts with the Olmecs and the peoples of Chiapas and their mutual interaction may have led to the growth of urban places in the Highlands. The outlines of this urban process are now particularly well identified in the Valley of Oaxaca, thanks to the important long-term research of archaeologists such as Kent Flannery, Joyce Marcus, and Richard Blanton.

These scholars have documented a similar trend towards complexity in Oaxaca as in the Gulf Coast. But whereas developments in the latter region led only to the relatively short-lived phase of the Olmecs, those in the Valley of Oaxaca gave rise, by 500 BC, to the first city in ancient Mexico: Monte Alban, and the first Mexican state a few centuries later.

27 View north over the great Zapotec capital of Monte Alban in the Valley of Oaxaca.

The principal precursor to Monte Alban in Oaxaca was the site of San Jose Mogote, lying in the northern arm of the Valley. Like San Lorenzo, San Jose Mogote was beginning to expand by 1350 BC. According to the Flannery team, 350 years later it had increased in size considerably, with a central zone of about 20 hectares and an overall occupation area perhaps as large as 70 hectares. The population in this larger area may have exceeded 700 souls. San Jose Mogote appears to have acted like a magnet, drawing in people from neighboring parts of the Valley. Many exotic trade goods were found at the site – such as stingray spines from the Pacific Ocean, used to rasp tongues or ears to draw blood during ceremonial rites. There were also specialized craft areas within the site, such as for the production of mirrors made from magnetite. It seems that some inhabitants of San Jose Mogote enjoyed a superior status and an ability to command exotic goods.

San Jose Mogote and Monte Alban

San Jose Mogote was the principal precursor to Monte Alban in the Valley of Oaxaca.

28 (*right*) The main plaza at Monte Alban, looking south.

29 (*below*) The ball court at Monte Alban. The ball game was played in ancient Mexico for at least 2,000 years. Compare ills. 3, 138–141.

30 (*below right*) The largest Rosario Phase (700–500 BC) public building at San Jose Mogote. The excavators report that the workman with the 2-meter stadia rod stands beside Structure 28, a plaster-surfaced adobe platform that once supported a large wattle-and-daub building with offerings under each of its four corners. Under the workman's feet lies Structure 19, a stone masonry platform whose fill contains a sequence of earlier structures, stratigraphically below Structure 28.

Within several centuries the town had grown even larger, with an estimated population of 1,000 people. The first substantial ceremonial architecture was constructed on top of high stone platforms, and monumental sculpture was being carved. The first definite evidence for the appearance of hieroglyphic writing and calendrics (a 260-day calendar) occurs between 600 and 500 BC.

The ancient Mexicans invented two basic calendars, the 260 day and the 365 day. The latter obviously has its origins in the observation of the solar year, while the former may have been related to an agricultural season, although its origins are less clear. Each calendar had day and month names, and when combined they produced a period of fifty-two years (260 × 365 days), the basic Mesoamerican cycle. The ancient Mexicans, particularly the Maya, also had a complex mathematical system based on the number "20" (instead of "10" which is so familiar to us today). The early glyphs in Oaxaca have been interpreted by the archaeologist Joyce Marcus as number and day glyphs relating to the 260-day calendar. The 365-day calendar was developed soon afterwards.

Sites in the other arms of the Valley of Oaxaca grew in size and complexity at the same time as San Jose Mogote, but none reached the same proportions. Richard Blanton argued some years ago that to forestall internecine warfare, to provide for common defence in the Valley against potential external threats, and to present a unified front to the outside world, the major powers in the three arms of the Valley, including San Jose Mogote, cooperatively established a central capital around 500 BC at the previously unoccupied juncture where all three territories met. This new site, or "disembedded capital," as Blanton called it, was Monte Alban. Because Blanton did not find evidence in his surveys for many large-scale manufacturing or workshop areas at the site, he concluded that Monte Alban was not the economic center of the Valley and its political power was not embedded in its economic importance. Brasilia, the political capital of modern-day Brazil, is a good example of this kind of "disembedded" center – founded as a neutral site away from other large competing centers such as Rio de Janeiro and Sao Paulo; another example is Canberra, the capital of Australia, which lies equidistant between the trading centers of Sydney and Melbourne.

Many archaeologists, however, have disagreed with Blanton's original formulation. One contention is that there were no strong external threats to the Valley of Oaxaca, and no obvious rivals to San

Reliefs, glyphs and calendars

31 Stela 3 and Stela 4 on the northeast corner of the great South Platform, Monte Alban, *c.* AD 250–450. Joyce Marcus interprets Stela 3 as a bound captive dressed as an animal, while Stela 4 shows a Zapotec ruler wielding a lance and standing on the symbol of a conquered territory. Glyphs can be seen to the left of Stela 3.

32 The ancient Mexican calendar, early evidence for which is found on Zapotec monuments, reached its zenith with the Maya. The 52-year cycle, created by the intermeshing of the 260-day calendar (left) and the 365-day calendar (right) is shown diagrammatically as a series of interlocking wheels and follows standard Maya notation.

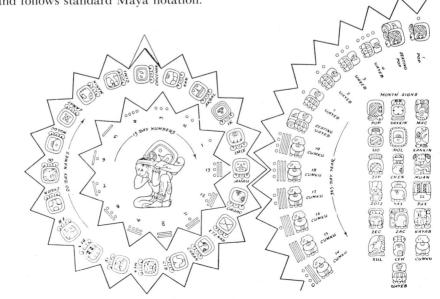

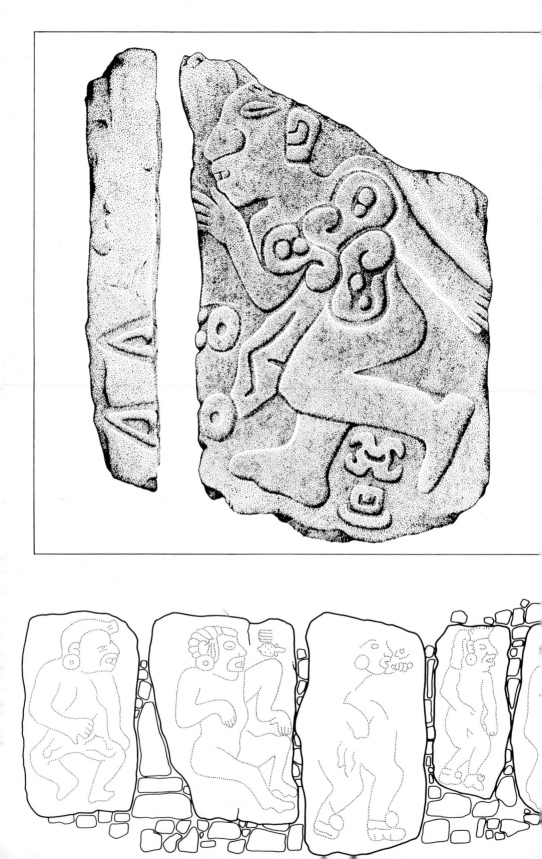

Danzante figures

Once thought to represent *danzantes* or "dancers," these powerful carvings are now believed to display the corpses of prisoners captured in battle. The tradition of building *danzante* monuments, which reached its height at Monte Alban, first began at San Jose Mogote.

33 (*far left*) A *danzante* figure on Monument 3, San Jose Mogote, dating to the later part of the Rosario Phase (600–500 BC).

34,35 Captive *danzante* figures as they were originally arranged on Structure L at Monte Alban, dating to between 500 and 200 BC. The glyphs in front of the figures' mouths in the lowest row may give their names.

Jose Mogote within the Valley at the time of Monte Alban's founding; therefore, the argument that the latter was established as a neutral site amidst warring centers has little strength. Among the most likely alternatives to the "disembedded capital" model is the hypothesis that Monte Alban was in fact established by San Jose Mogote to advance its preeminent position in the Valley of Oaxaca.

While the "disembedded capital" hypothesis may be debated, the position and new dominance of Monte Alban after 500 BC is unarguable. The number of its inhabitants during the first few centuries of growth reached probably as many as 5,000 people. Based on this expanding central capital, the Zapotec state may have been formed during this period, which is known archaeologically as Monte Alban I. It was certainly present by Monte Alban II, from 200 BC to AD 250.

The new role that Monte Alban began to play is reflected in the carving of hundreds of *danzante* figures. Michael Coe and Joyce Marcus have both argued convincingly that these naked figures, which used to be called dancers, can be identified as representations of captives obtained by Monte Alban during battles. Moreover, the forerunners of these figures have been found at Monte Alban's predecessor, San Jose Mogote.

Based on his settlement surveys of domestic houses and surface features, Blanton contends that Monte Alban's population, which had reached at least 15,000 by 200 BC, was fed in part by the increase in small-scale irrigation agriculture in the Valley. Although a large proportion of the population of the Valley of Oaxaca resided at Monte Alban, the number of inhabitants in the surrounding villages and towns also began to increase dramatically.

Strong evidence for the consolidation of the Zapotec state based on Monte Alban can be found during the Monte Alban II period. Large palace structures – in which it is inferred that the ruling elite of the city lived and administered the Valley of Oaxaca and neighboring zones – were built, and hieroglyphic texts (as yet only partially deciphered), that refer to specific tribute-paying and conquered places in the Zapotec state, were inscribed.

Monte Alban reached its zenith during the next period, when it apparently was able to hold the expanding power of Teotihuacan – lying to the north in the Basin of Mexico – at bay. There is no evidence of any Teotihuacan conquest of Monte Alban; instead, there are some indications, particularly the finding of what has been interpreted as a Oaxacan enclave or *barrio* at Teotihuacan, of cordial relations.

36 This jade bat mask from Monte Alban II was found in an offering on the Main Plaza.

37 The ceramic figure known as "The Scribe of Cuilapan," Monte Alban II.

Although for the next 200 years, between AD 250 and 450, Monte Alban did not expand, it was able – more-or-less – to hold its own, and in the period from AD 450 to 700 it reached a peak population of nearly 25,000 people.

At its apogee, the city must have been an impressive place: the Main Plaza surrounded by large buildings; all three hilltops on which the site was built showing dense occupation; terraces on the hill slopes filled with houses; fifteen residential subdivisions with their own plazas; and elaborate tombs for the elite. The Main Plaza was situated on top of a flattened hill, with a magnificent view of the Valley below. It was an immense, open, paved area, defined by a series of stone buildings including temples, a large ball court, and a peculiar arrow-shaped structure (J) which, it has been argued – on the basis of its orientation – may have been used, in part, for astronomical purposes, although it almost certainly had other functions too.

In the eighth century AD, the Zapotec state crumbled and Monte Alban diminished in power and size. Its population at this time was reduced to less than 5,000 people. Blanton believes that the Valley was fragmented into a number of "petty states," of which Monte Alban was one. The reasons for Monte Alban's decline are not entirely clear, although the fall of Teotihuacan at about the same time (see Chapter Four), with the consequent cessation of external threat, may have led to a questioning of the Valley-wide support for the great center, while the loss of long-distance trade with Teotihuacan may also have had negative economic consequences. Perhaps its administrative functions were then divided among many smaller-scale societies.

Teotihuacan: Metropolis in the Valley of Mexico

While Monte Alban was flourishing, urban centers also began to develop to the north, in the Valley of Mexico. One of the most important and impressive cities of ancient Mexico was Teotihuacan, situated some 40 kilometers northeast of modern-day Mexico City. The visitor to Teotihuacan cannot help but be awed by the massiveness of the city's major buildings; the careful planning of the urban center's layout; and the extent of the dense building and occupation. Visitors in the past must have felt the same way, because the express intent of Teotihuacan's designers seems to have been to overwhelm both resident and visitor alike. The design was to glorify the gods of the Teotihuacanos and to sanctify the religious significance of the city and its landscape. It also acted as a magnet to surrounding populations. We know from our own times that people tend to be lured toward cities. They are seen as places of wealth, excitement, and opportunity.

TIME: Around AD 500

PLACE: Valley of Mexico

CIVILIZATION: Teotihuacan

The merchant approaches the great metropolis from the south, via the Puebla area. He is following a road that leads to the city through the Teotihuacan Valley. The sun beats down on his head as he hurries across the parched uplands, with cacti dotted far into the distance. He catches his first glimpse of the city while still some way off, the huge pyramids of the Sun and Moon looming on the horizon. He stops for a moment to rest.

Although the merchant knows Teotihuacan well he is always stunned on his periodic visits by the sheer immensity of the city. On the outskirts he passes large expanses of irrigated fields. Canals connect the field systems with the river that flows through the valley. Now, instead of just meeting the occasional traveler, the merchant has to thread his way among all the other people making their way to and from the city: merchants, pilgrims, visitors from distant towns and cities, and laborers carrying obsidian from the mines. Everyone is on foot. Reaching the city center the merchant is directed at once to the quarters reserved for visiting traders. He offers silent thanks for his safe arrival to the god who watches over merchants on their travels.

Next morning the merchant walks to the great avenue [the Street of the Dead]. He finds it hard to imagine that there could be a more magnificent sight anywhere in the world. Looking up the street to the north, he sees a huge pyramid [the Moon] surmounted by a temple, while an even higher one [the Sun] dominates the landscape off to the east. The great stairway leading to the top of the nearest pyramid is crowded with people; on the summit a priest is conducting ceremonies to honor Tlaloc, the god of rain. The merchant sees a bound prisoner held captive: it seems that the ceremony is to include a sacrifice. Incense burners are lit, and the fragrant smoke wafts towards the skies. Although he calls the rain god by a different name, the merchant knows how crucial these ceremonies are to ensure adequate rain for the crops.

Grandiose multi-roomed stone buildings line the great avenue. The merchant hurries past them towards an immense marketplace that dominates one side of the street. Near the entrance he passes an elaborate complex – completely walled in – that houses the palace and temple of the ruler of Teotihuacan.

The merchant calls at one of the buildings that serves as the office of the bureaucrat responsible for administering the market. He is given permission to trade at Teotihuacan subject to the rules established and maintained by the state. Entering the huge marketplace he stands for a moment, his senses assaulted by the crowds, the noise and the color. Traders are everywhere, shouting, bargaining. Sellers call out their wares. Every color of the rainbow seems to be on display: multi-colored maize; red and yellow peppers; green, gray, and black obsidian. The market is highly organized, with different products sold in distinct areas. Obsidian is confined to one large corner, while pottery is sold nearby, with different stands reserved for cooking vessels, water jars, and serving plates. Foodstuffs can be bought in another corner, and clothing towards the center of the market.

With an experienced eye the merchant examines the various kinds of obsidian available. He barters for some pieces of the highly demanded, green obsidian from the nearby Navajas mines. It is sold in the shape of carefully prepared cores that have been chipped from larger chunks mined at Navajas. The merchant pays for them with a few cacao beans and with several well-woven and decorated cotton tunics for which his town is famous. He had obtained the cacao beans (which act as a currency) for some other woven goods he had sold en route. Back in his town, he will trade the obsidian to several craftspeople who will strike sharp blades from the cores. The merchant chats to the obsidian seller and is invited to visit the workshop later that day.

The obsidian-working neighborhood near the marketplace is only one of many in this capital of the obsidian trade. To get there, the merchant has to pass row upon row of similarly designed apartment compounds. The distinctive Teotihuacan architecture, with its sloping lower walls and inset panels, is everywhere, as are the lively, multi-colored murals depicting gods and complex symbols whose meaning the merchant can scarcely comprehend.

Most of the obsidian workshops produce tools from both green and gray obsidian. The noise of chipping is incessant as knappers, squatting on the ground with chunks of obsidian in front of them, strike blades off the cores. The obsidian seller shows the merchant around his workshop; he is impressed by the great skill with which the cores are prepared and the quality of the product. Certainly, these blades will be in great demand.

Their business concluded, the seller invites the merchant to join his family for a meal. Like most of the obsidian workers, they live in an apartment compound adjacent to the workshop. With the meal over, and feeling replete, the merchant sets out on his homeward journey.

Central Mexico: Teotihuacan

Like sites in the Valley of Oaxaca, those in the Basin of Mexico were also in contact with developing Mexican groups, including the Olmecs, exporting obsidian and other goods to them and receiving in return finished craft goods. Intensive surface surveys throughout the Basin, undertaken over a period of years by the archaeologist William Sanders and his colleagues, have uncovered a fascinating series of settlement patterns covering many centuries. These surveys have revealed a large number of sites that show a long history of population growth and movement.

In the centuries following 1000 BC, the rapidly expanding population of the Basin of Mexico began to concentrate mainly in two places. These sites, Cuicuilco in the southwest corner of the Basin and Teotihuacan in a side valley in the northeast part, soon grew to the size of towns. By 300 BC, Cuicuilco (which only a few years ago lay outside

38 The Street of the Dead at Teotihuacan, with the Pyramid of the Sun
to the left.

the southern border of modern Mexico City but now lies well within its
urban zone) may have had a population of more than 10,000 people.
But Teotihuacan soon outstripped it in size and importance and
between 300 and 100 BC came to dominate the Basin of Mexico; soon
thereafter many other parts of Mesoamerica also came under its
control.

Teotihuacan's rapid growth over these two centuries, when its
population was probably in the tens of thousands, may have been aided
in part by a natural phenomenon which helped to diminish Cuicuilco's
influence and ultimately to destroy it. Volcanic eruptions in the
southwest part of the Basin first covered much of the agricultural land
surrounding Cuicuilco, thus crippling the economy of the city, and
ultimately covered the site itself, although their exact timing is as yet
unclear. The *pedregal*, or lava zones, of Mexico City are the modern

remains of these eruptions. With the loss of its principal competitor, Teotihuacan, which may well have been getting the better of the rivalry anyway, underwent a spectacular growth spurt as it consolidated its economic, political, and religious authority over Central Mexico.

By 100 BC, it is estimated that Teotihuacan's population may have exceeded 40,000 people. Six hundred years later this figure had probably tripled to 120,000, and may even have been as high as 200,000. The archaeologist René Millon, a leading authority on Teotihuacan, has noted that by the mid-first millennium AD, when, for example, Paris and London were relatively insignificant centers, Teotihuacan was one of the largest cities in the world.

Even today, tourists are staggered not by the aesthetic beauty of the site, as they might be by the Maya city of Palenque, but by its scale and immensity: the 600 pyramids, the 2,000 apartment compounds all built to similar plans, the numerous workshop areas, and the great market compound. Yet the scale of building was not something that developed slowly over time as the city grew in size and power. The most striking features of Teotihuacan, its careful planning and the overwhelming size of some of its structures, were among the initial developments of the city: the great Pyramid of the Sun, for instance, was built early on in Teotihuacan's history, while the city's grid plan – radiating out from the 5-kilometer-long Street of the Dead – was laid out well before the construction of most of its great buildings. Referring to the overall planning of Teotihuacan, and particularly to the huge structures that line the Street of the Dead, Millon eloquently states:

The bold self-confidence manifest in the planning and execution of this grand design points to an authority, be it individual or collective, that had an unchallenged prestige, with an ability to motivate masses of people and the power to mobilize and direct workers and resources on a scale that until then was without precedent in Middle America. The imposition of monumentality of this magnitude on the city's vital central avenue represents a spectacular realization in stone of the values and goals of its builders, no less than the monumental use of public space in imperial Peking, ancient Rome, Paris, Versailles, Washington, or the contemporary Manhattan skyline.[7]

The reasons for the rise of Teotihuacan in the side valley leading into the large Valley of Mexico are clearly complex, but four principal factors must have been involved. One was the presence of an important, nearby source of obsidian. Second, the Teotihuacan Valley

39,40 **Cuicuilco** Once a great rival of Teotihuacan in the Basin of Mexico, the city of Cuicuilco – with its temple platform (*above* and *below*) – may have been destroyed by volcanic eruptions some 2,000 years ago.

Teotihuacan architecture

41 A courtyard near the center of the city, with the Pyramid of the Sun in the background.

42,43 Teotihuacan architecture often featured the distinctive sloping *talud* with the vertical *tablero* above (*right*) as seen in the construction of a small pyramid located within the citadel (*far right*).

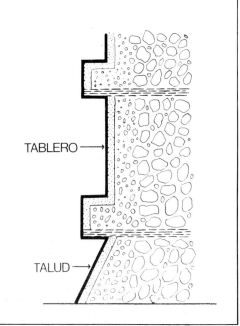

TABLERO →

TALUD →

sat astride a natural trade route from the Basin of Mexico to the east (towards the Gulf Coast), and to the south. Third, ecologically, the valley had much potential for intensive agriculture through the use of irrigation. And fourth, from very early in its history, before its major urban growth, the site of Teotihuacan apparently had great religious significance.

This religious importance of the site is supported by the discovery of a cave below the Pyramid of the Sun, with offerings in one of the rooms. The cave, which perhaps was seen as an entrance to the underworld, could have served as a religious shrine that helped to attract people to the Teotihuacan Valley during the formative days of the city's development. Teotihuacan's importance as a pilgrimage site during its apogee may, therefore, have had a long history.

All these factors may well have reinforced each other to provide the thrust that launched Teotihuacan on its meteoric rise to prominence. While the city's religious importance may have been an early population lure, the need for labor to mine the obsidian, manufacture obsidian tools and other goods, transport these items to distant markets, work the fields, dig and maintain the canals for intensive cultivation, and construct the great buildings that helped attract both pilgrims and merchants must have been a paramount consideration to the rulers of Teotihuacan. Voluntary immigration may have sufficed during the city's early days, but there is some inferential evidence that, as Teotihuacan's power grew, people were coerced to move there. One scholar has compared the city to a vacuum that forcibly sucked up all the population in the Basin of Mexico. According to this line of argument, by enveloping the regionally available population, Teotihuacan not only made sure that its rapidly expanding labor needs were met, it also prevented the possible development of rival centers of any size or importance in the large zone surrounding the site. The decline of neighboring villages and towns at this time is used to support this line of argument.

After the time of Christ, Teotihuacan began to extend its influence beyond the Basin of Mexico. The nature of this spread is still not completely clear. It may, in part, have involved military conquest, as some have argued – on the basis of Teotihuacan architectural style, symbolism, and artifacts – is the case at the distant site of Kaminaljuyu, located within the bounds of modern Guatemala City. Others, however, have contended that Teotihuacan influence was more peaceful. Kaminaljuyu is strategically situated near a major obsidian

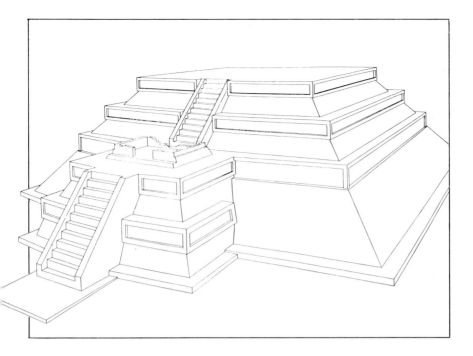

44 Strong Teotihuacan influence can be seen at the Highland Maya site of Kaminaljuyu, on the outskirts of modern-day Guatemala City, as in the building known as Structure B-4, shown here in a reconstruction drawing.

source, and it is conceivable, but still a matter of speculation, that Teotihuacan tried to obtain a monopoly over this economically crucial material. In addition, Kaminaljuyu also sat astride a principal trade route for cacao, the bean that was used as money in ancient Mexico. Clearly it would have been economically desirable for Teotihuacan to have some degree of influence over the site.

In other instances, Teotihuacan's influence may have been economic, political, or religious, without any active military coercion. Its presence was felt, for example, in both the Gulf Coast region and the Maya Lowlands. In the Lowlands, we have archaeological evidence at the great site of Tikal in Guatemala of Teotihuacan-influenced pottery and other artifacts, Teotihuacan figures carved on a monument, and typically Teotihuacan architecture featuring its distinctive sloped *talud-tablero* style with vertical framed panels directly above sloping basal aprons. Moreover, research on the hieroglyphic inscriptions at Tikal suggests that Teotihuacan influence at Tikal may have been initiated through an elite individual, known as "Curl Nose," who may have come from Kaminaljuyu and married into the fledgling ruling dynasty of Tikal. Other scholars see "Curl Nose" as a Maya who symbolically aligned himself with Kaminaljuyu (and Teotihuacan).

Teotihuacan also maintained relations with Monte Alban, although it never controlled Oaxaca. As noted above, a Oaxacan residential unit (or *barrio* as it is known) was found at Teotihuacan and has been interpreted as a Oaxacan embassy or merchants' residence.

Clearly, the nature of Teotihuacan's expansion in ancient Mexico was complex and varied. Although it secured total control of the Basin of Mexico and perhaps more distant locales of strategic importance, Teotihuacan does not appear to have controlled a unified empire. Its mercantile influence, however, spread widely through parts of Mesoamerica. Yet even in this case, the amount and importance of far-flung Teotihuacan trade is a matter of much debate. Along with traded goods came symbols of Teotihuacan's religious system, although the extent of its prosletyzing activities is unknown. It may be that mercantile and religious expansion were inextricably bound together.

By AD 500, Teotihuacan had reached the height of its power. Covering an area of more than 20 square kilometers, the huge urban center dominated ancient Mexico. Within the next two centuries, however, there are indications that its influence had begun to wane. Some of the control over the distant reaches of the area was lost, and the city record indicates that times were tense. Millon points out that "The military is most prominently represented at Teotihuacan [between AD 650 and 750]. . . . This may be both a symptom of difficulty and a cause of it."[8]

Sometime around the middle of the eighth century AD, the site collapsed. It has been suggested that the central zone was ritually destroyed and burned. Although a relatively sizeable population remained in the city after AD 750, it was much reduced from the 120,000 to 200,000 people who had previously inhabited the site. Teotihuacan's days of glory became only a memory, although the reasons for its decline still elude archaeologists.

While numerous hypotheses have been advanced to explain Teotihuacan's demise, none has proved really satisfactory. Two of the most popular have been climatic deterioration, such as a drying up of the environment, or invasion – either by semi-nomadic groups from the north and west, or by peoples from newly burgeoning cities like Cholula. While both are possible, they do not account for the causes of the great center's vulnerability to such events. Perhaps the latter can

45 Stela 4 at Tikal, dating to AD 380, depicts "Curl Nose," possibly an outsider from Kaminaljuyu who married into the local ruling dynasty at Tikal, or a Maya who adopted non-Maya trappings.

Masks, paintings and statuary

46 (*left*) Giant stone sculpture of Chalchiutlicue, goddess of water, originally situated near the Pyramid of the Moon at Teotihuacan.

47 (*below*) Wall paintings not only provided decoration but were an important means of communication in Teotihuacan. This illustration shows what art historian Arthur Miller has interpreted as a jaguar blowing a plumed conch shell.

48 (*right*) Ceramic incense burner in the form of a temple within which resides the mask of a god.

be found in the archaeologist George Cowgill's argument that a series of bad decisions by an increasingly inefficient bureaucracy propelled the city to the brink of disaster. At the moment, it is not clear whether one of these factors, or possibly a combination of all three, was responsible for the decline of Teotihuacan.

CHAPTER FIVE

The Southern Maya Sites of Cerros and Palenque

While the Valleys of Mexico and Oaxaca were witnessing the rise of urban centers just before the time of Christ, so were the Maya Lowlands. One of the most important sites at this time was the strategically located town of Cerros in Belize, where recent research has been undertaken by Southern Methodist University.

TIME: 25 BC

PLACE: Cerros, on the eastern edge of the Southern Maya Lowlands

CIVILIZATION: Maya

The priest has been traveling downriver by dugout canoe for many days from his home at Lamanai on the New River. Entering a broad, calm bay, the paddlers begin to pull towards the near shore and soon, in the distance, the priest can see a dock jutting out into the bay. The forest along the shoreline has been cleared here, and a large acropolis looms above the landscape, part of the town of Cerros. The priest, a venerable religious figure, has come to Cerros to participate in a ceremony dedicating a newly constructed pyramid.

The canoe ties up at the busy jetty – where trade goods are being loaded and unloaded from other canoes – and the passengers disembark. The priest looks around in astonishment. It has been many years since he was last in Cerros and he finds it difficult to take in all the changes. Gone is the relatively small, thriving village at the mouth of the river. In its place is a huge stone platform topped by a tall temple, with beautiful painted stucco masks flanking the main stairway. Several other sizeable structures are being built, with numerous residences clustering near them. Hundreds of laborers are cutting immense limestone blocks and setting them in place, while other groups of workers haul smaller rocks to use inside the structures. The work is fast and efficient.

A delegation, including the head priest of Cerros, meets the priest at the jetty. He receives a formal but warm welcome and, after a meal and some rest, is shown the resplendent new monuments in the town. At the recently built acropolis the priest's host explains how they had razed to the ground the old village with its perishable houses and erected the large stone structures in its place. With great pride he points out one of the finer details – a depiction of the morning star [what we now call the planet Venus] on a recently completed stucco mask adorning a new building.

A wide canal surrounding the central zone is being constructed to bring water to a new agricultural area. Smaller feeder canals are also being dug to intensify the cultivation and provide more food for the town's growing population – as well as for the workers from surrounding communities brought to Cerros to help with its massive building program. New wood and thatch houses have been built around the fields to accommodate the growing number of farmers.

Impressed as he is by all the changes, the priest recalls that within his lifetime his own town of Lamanai has also undergone a transformation. Both places have benefited from the same growth in trade with distant towns and villages. But whereas Lamanai has participated in this trade mainly as a producer of crops such as cacao and cotton, or as a consumer of materials like obsidian, because of its critical location Cerros's role has been as middleman in the trading routes. The priest can see the town's major imports on several storage platforms – salt from the coasts to the north, and obsidian and jade from the south. As demand for these goods has increased in recent years, trade has intensified, and Cerros's size, importance, and wealth has grown concomitantly. The priest recalls from his journey that at least some of the rising demand for new products must be coming from the developing villages in the regions near the river.

Filled with all the new sights, and tired from his long journey, the priest retires to rest for the coming ceremonies.

49 Stucco masks flanking the main stairway of structure 5C-2nd at Cerros.

The Southern Maya Lowlands until AD 600

Scholars traditionally held that civilization developed in the Maya Lowlands at the beginning of the Classic Period, the start of which was linked to the carving of the first full hieroglyphic calendrical date, just prior to AD 300. But a host of new investigations, including field surveys, excavations, and research on hieroglyphic decipherment, have now caused major revisions in this view – and many others – of the ancient Maya.

It seems certain that the Maya began to live in small settled villages, supported by the cultivation of maize and other crops, certainly as early as 1000 BC and perhaps much earlier. With abundant forests available for clearing and cultivation, there is no evidence for population pressure on the land at this time or for many centuries. Settlement surveys do indicate, however, that throughout the first

50 The great Central Plaza at Tikal, Guatemala. Many of the stelae in the plaza were removed from their original locations and reset in the plaza at the time of Tikal's demise in the ninth century AD.

millennium BC the size of the population gradually increased and that new lowland zones were colonized. By 300 BC (the beginning of the Late Preclassic Period), the Maya world began to experience the kind of development that had already begun in Oaxaca and Central Mexico.

Field research at sites such as Cuello, Cerros, and Lamanai in Belize; Nakbe and El Mirador in Guatemala; and Komchen in Northern Yucatan, when combined with the excavation data from the important sites of Tikal and Dzibilchaltun, indicate that the beginnings of urban growth in the Maya Lowlands can be placed at around 300 BC and monumental construction even before that – many years earlier than had previously been supposed. Research at these sites has shown that, within the first several centuries of the Late Preclassic Period, highly decorated, large-scale structures were built, experiments with

51 A reconstruction of the immense Late Preclassic architecture of the Southern Lowland site of El Mirador, Guatemala.

intensive agriculture were initiated, and extensive long-distance trade networks were developed. A number of new sites were also founded as the once-vacant Lowlands became populated and the number of inhabitants at the already established sites increased. Soon thereafter the skill of hieroglyphic writing became established and spread in the Lowlands, and calendrics and astronomy flourished. Although lowland Maya writing certainly derived from developments in Oaxaca and the Maya Highlands, it quickly gained its own unique complexity.

Reasons for this Late Preclassic cultural expansion are a matter of much debate, but the rise in population, territorial crowding, increased conflict, and possible migrations from the Highlands, either singly or in combination, are some of the most plausible hypotheses that have been argued in the recent literature.

By AD 300, some of the early centers of Maya civilization, such as Cerros and El Mirador, went into decline, perhaps as a result of changing trade patterns; others, like Tikal – that were already complex sites – continued to expand. In addition, a number of previously minor centers such as Copan also grew in size and importance. Maya civilization entered the Classic Period, and thrived throughout the Lowlands.

Palenque

While Teotihuacan and Monte Alban were flourishing in the Mexican Highlands, Classic Maya civilization reached its zenith in the Lowlands of the greater Yucatan peninsula. Teotihuacan had some economic and political impact on the development of the ancient Maya, but by the end of the sixth century AD its influence had waned. Coincident with the shrinkage of Teotihuacan's influence in Mesoamerica, a number of major Classic Maya centers increased in power and began to vie for control of territory, people, and resources. One of the most successful of these cities was Palenque, lying near the western frontier of the Maya Lowlands. Under the leadership of its great ruler Pacal in particular, whose name-glyph has been directly associated with the rich tomb beneath the Temple of the Inscriptions there, Palenque became the dominant center in its region, and one of the most influential in the Lowlands. Through military raids and marriage alliances it was able to extend its control over a wide area. While Pacal built the largest and most famous structure at Palenque, the Temple of the Inscriptions, to house his tomb, the temples that have been labeled the Temples of the Cross, Foliated Cross, and Sun, and the palace complex, were all built during the reigns of two of his sons.

TIME: AD 684

PLACE: Palenque, the western border of the Southern Maya Lowlands

CIVILIZATION: Maya

As the architect watches the body of his ruler, Pacal, being carried up the steps of the great temple he had designed some years earlier, his pride is mixed with much sadness. Pacal's strength and intelligence had given the city great power, wealth, and influence, and had provided the resources that enabled the architect to create this magnificent structure. Early in his reign Pacal had decided to build a temple to house the tomb – a large chamber with an immense sarcophagus – where he would be enshrined after his death. He envisaged the new pyramid-temple as the central focus of Palenque, which had already grown under his skillful leadership from a relatively minor town to a sizeable city. Palenque had a magnificent location, nestling in tropical rainforest near the foot of a mountain range, and the new structure would dominate this setting.

The architect, who was a member of an elite family related to Pacal, and who as a young man had already shown evidence of a quick and imaginative mind, had been given the signal honor of taking over the supervision of the building of Pacal's great monument after the original architect had died.

The most difficult parts of the enterprise had been the organization of labor to build the temple and pyramid; the quarrying of limestone; the shaping of building blocks with chert axes; and the moving of the blocks from the quarry to the building site. Careful estimates of the number and size of blocks had been made, as well as fine calculations as to the dimensions of the stones that would make up the corbeled vaults inside the building. Meanwhile, huge quantities of cement and plaster had been mixed, and trees felled and prepared for beams, lintels, and the scaffolding needed to support the vaults temporarily during construction. Other trees had also been brought into the city for firewood to burn the lime to make cement. To complicate matters further, everything had had to be timed to the agricultural cycle to avoid heavy rains during certain phases of the construction.

Even with the huge number of laborers involved, the project had taken more than fifteen years. This had partly been due to the size and elaborateness of the structure, and partly because many of the workers were only available for some of the year. The rest of the time they had had to labor in the fields. Only the specialists were able to work on the project full-time, the most important of these being the masons. Although their work was not as obvious as that of other artisans, the masons had the critical job of preparing the cement with exactly the right proportions of lime and other constituents.

Having built the tomb and the pyramidal base the next critical part of the construction had been the center wall of the temple. The architect had personally supervised this phase, because it was crucial that this wall should be built accurately and the cement aged correctly if the subsequently constructed outer walls and the completed vaults for the front and back rooms were to be successful.

Even after the basic structure had been erected there was still a vast amount of work left undone. Pacal had gotten the finest artisans to sculpt the stucco figures on the temple, and superb carvers to work on the lid of the sarcophagus and other carved stones. Space in the inscriptions had been reserved to inscribe the date of his death. But the crowning touch, the architect thinks to himself, as the funeral procession reaches the top of the stairs and begins to move inside the temple, had been the commissioning of a jade mask to be placed over Pacal's face in his tomb. Pacal had ordered his merchants to obtain the finest jades from distant sources, and had then had the most skilled craftsmen laboriously carve each piece with string and sand, and polish it with stone tools to achieve the beautiful mosaic effect.

Soon, thinks the architect, his mind snapping back to the present, the priests will place the jade mosaic over Pacal's face as a death mask. He will be adorned with his favorite jade bracelets and necklace, as well as other ornaments, and several of his servants will be sacrificed to the glory of the gods. Then the workers will carefully lower the giant sarcophagus lid into place over Pacal's body, and the tomb will be sealed.

52 A cutaway view of the Temple of the Inscriptions at Palenque. From the sanctuary above a secret internal stairway leads to the sarcophagus chamber of Pacal, located at ground-level.

The Southern Maya Lowlands from AD 600 to 800

It used to be thought that the Maya in the Classic Period (AD 300–800) developed in isolation from their neighbors, their lives focused on non-urban ceremonial centers. These centers were supposedly run by a priestly elite who erected carved monuments that were full of esoteric hieroglyphic inscriptions concerned with astronomy and calendrics. The centers lived in peace with one another and were supported by scattered peasants who practiced slash-and-burn (swidden) agriculture, with maize as the major crop. The overall impression was one of both cultural homogeneity and uniqueness.

Over the past three decades, as new data have poured in, most of the tenets of the traditional view have had to be revised. Far from being static and homogeneous, the many centuries of the Classic Period are revealed as a time of dynamic change. Scholars now recognize that the Maya centers housed large populations and that a variety of intensive forms of agriculture, including terracing and the reclamation of swampland, were undertaken to support these cities. Although the settlement was not as dense as that in the Highlands, many sites had 5,000 to 10,000 occupants, and a few of the largest, such as Tikal, Caracol, and Calakmul, have been estimated to have had populations

53 The Palace at Palenque, with its three-story tower.

in excess of 40,000.

Tikal is located in the jungle Lowlands of the Peten in modern-day Guatemala. A vast amount of construction was undertaken by the Maya elite there between about 300 BC and AD 800, including a series of tall, steep pyramids topped by temples and large "palace" complexes. Research at Tikal conducted by the University of Pennsylvania Museum over a fifteen-year period has been instrumental in changing scholarly views of the nature of Classic Maya civilization.

Archaeologists also now realize that the Maya had important contacts with both close and distant neighbors, as we saw in Chapter Four, and that they were far from peaceful as had previously been believed. There is ample evidence in Maya art of captive figures, such as the murals at the site of Bonampak, that show that raiding and warfare were common occurrences. Hieroglyphic inscriptions also indicate the importance of combat, while earthworks and moats around and between sites have been inferred to have had defensive functions. New research at sites adjacent to the Pasion River has further bolstered the view that intersite raiding played a significant role among the Classic Maya.

Classic Maya art

54 (*left*) Copy of a wall painting from Room 2, Structure 1, at the Southern Lowland site of Bonampak, *c.* AD 790. Captives from a raid are being tortured and lie at the feet of a Bonampak noble and his richly clad retinue.

55 (*opposite below*) An engraved stone from Bonampak, dating to the beginning of the Late Classic period. A Maya noble is seated on a throne with three individuals of lesser status before him.

56 (*below left*) Stela 31 from Tikal depicts the ruler "Stormy Sky" in AD 445. The style of the monument lends some weight to the suggestion that Teotihuacan had connections with Tikal, perhaps indirectly via Teotihuacan-influenced Kaminaljuyu.

57 (*below right*) Like the mural from Bonampak opposite, Stela 12 from Piedras Negras, Guatemala, also shows a ruler with captives at his feet. This monument dates to AD 795, just prior to the fall of the site.

The Maya nobility at Palenque

58 (*left*) Palenque is famous for its beautiful stucco sculpture as in this head of a Maya noble, found beneath the Temple of the Inscriptions.

59 (*below*) Life-size jade mosaic death mask of Pacal, found in the sarcophagus of the Temple of the Inscriptions and dated to AD 683. The jade pieces were once fixed to a wooden backing, while the eyes are of shell and obsidian.

60 (*right*) Carved relief of a Maya noble at Palenque.

Another important discovery is that the hieroglyphic inscriptions on Maya monuments, architecture, and ceramics were not concerned solely with esoteric information but rather contain historical, political, and social data of great interest. Perhaps the most important breakthrough was made twenty-five years ago by the archaeologist and epigrapher Tatiana Proskouriakoff who found a series of patterns on the monuments of Piedras Negras that she was able to interpret as the dates of accession of a sequence of rulers at the site. For example, Proskouriakoff was able to detail a sequence of six rulers whose dynasty held sway at Piedras Negras for 174 years with individual reigns of 35, 47, 42, 28, 5, and 17 years. She was even able to point out that there was a dynastic dispute over the accession of the fifth ruler in AD 756 and that the ruler from the powerful site of Yaxchilan, about 40 kilometers away, intervened.

At Tikal, scholars have identified the founding of the Jaguar Paw dynasty by the beginning of the fourth century AD and have detailed a series of successions including "Curl Nose," mentioned earlier, who married into the Jaguar Paw lineage in AD 378, and his son "Stormy Sky," who ascended to power at Tikal in AD 426 and is depicted on the famous Stela 31. Teotihuacan influence at Tikal at this time has been identified through analysis of the motifs on the monuments, and examination of the artifacts in the tombs of these two rulers.

Following up on Proskouriakoff's leads, as well as on the finding by the epigrapher Heinrich Berlin that particular glyphs (now called "emblem glyphs") could be associated with specific sites, scholars have pieced together the dynastic histories of a number of sites. Combined with new linguistic advances in the decipherment of the whole hieroglyphic system made by a host of researchers, including the linguist Floyd Lounsbury and the epigrapher Linda Schele, these new findings have led to the uncovering of large quantities of new data about the activities of the Classic upper class, the births, accessions, and deaths of particular rulers, their attempts at military and political expansion, and the marriage alliances forged among ruling families from different cities. Recent decipherments have also given valuable insights into ancient Maya religion and religious practices. Understandings of Classic Maya civilization, particularly its elite aspects, have thus grown significantly, although care must be taken not to take all the inscriptions as literal truths – Maya rulers may have been prone to exaggerate their accomplishments and those of their predecessors and perhaps try to rewrite history.

CHAPTER SIX

Uxmal and the Northern Maya Lowlands

Within a century or so of Pacal's death, most of the major Classic Maya centers in the Southern Lowlands went into decline, and many were abandoned. At roughly the same time, in the ninth century AD, the hilly Puuc region emerged as the principal population center in the north. Some of the triumphs in Maya architecture were built at Puuc region sites such as Kabah, Sayil, and Labna. But the largest and best-known Puuc site is Uxmal, located about 80 kilometers southwest of the modern city of Merida, capital of Yucatan.

TIME: AD 900

PLACE: Uxmal, Puuc region of the Northern Maya Lowlands

CIVILIZATION: Maya

Despite the heat the ball player straps on his bulky belt, hip pads, and knee pads of cotton and leather that both tradition and commonsense demand. Ball players have dressed in similar ways for nearly 2,000 years; the heavy equipment provides much-needed protection against the hard rubber ball. On special occasions the players also wear belts and pads made of carved stone, but they never play in them.

The ball player is related to the ruler of Uxmal and lives in a house that reflects his high status and wealth. It has stone walls, a vaulted stone roof, and four rooms. The two rooms at the back are sleeping quarters and the front rooms are the living areas. The kitchen is in a separate thatch-roofed structure, while a large underground cistern holds the family's water supply. Limestone for such construction purposes is quarried locally.

As the hour for the game approaches an acolyte arrives to lead the ball player to the main temple in the center of the city for the ceremonies that will precede the ball game. The player pushes back the fear of death that always grips him at this moment, for he knows that losing players may be sacrificed at the end of the game. All the dwellings they pass – whether luxurious homes or poorer wooden ones with thatched roofs – are on raised platforms from one to several meters high. The number of buildings on each platform varies, as do the sizes of the surrounding garden plots where fruits and vegetables such as beans and squashes are grown, but today the player notices none of these things.

The main temple [the Pyramid of the Magician] toward which they are heading is built on a great oval foundation. The ball player and the other players from Uxmal and the neighboring city of Kabah slowly climb the steep steps up to the temple. As this is not a major festival, the ruler of Uxmal is not among the players but instead is represented by members of the city's elite families.

The sweet smell of *copal*, a resin used in ceramic incense burners, fills the air. Priests meet the players at the main door of the temple and prayers are offered to the rain and maize gods asking for plentiful rain during the summer months, and for a bountiful harvest.

Priests and players then process from the temple toward the acropolis where the great palace of the ruler of Uxmal [the Palace of the Governors] is situated. Before the ruler joins the head of the procession he ritually draws some of his own blood to honor and glorify the gods.

They process toward the ball court that lies between the acropolis and a quadrangle with elaborate friezes on the upper façades [the Nunnery] where some of the elite live and work. The areas between these various buildings are paved with white plaster, while the structures themselves are coated with plaster and stucco and painted a wide variety of colors. Because of the careful city planning, the center alley of the ball court is aligned with the large vaulted entry to the quadrangle. Owing to the planned foreshortened perspective, the raised east range of the quadrangle gives the false impression of being the second storey of the front range. Although the ball player has seen all these sights many times before they never fail to impress him.

The priests and elite climb the stairways on the back walls of the ball court to sit in specially constructed buildings on the sides. From here they can look down and watch the game. The players take their places at opposite ends of the court, the two principal players on each side standing in the alley and the remaining players in the end zones. The large hard ball, made from the sap of a rubber tree, is produced.

The object of the game is to hit the ball through the rings, carved with hieroglyphic inscriptions, that are set high in the vertical walls forming the two parallel sides of the court. Each team aims for one of the rings. The playing area is the narrow alley formed by low sloping platforms attached to the bottom of the main walls. The ball must be hit by a player's body and not by his hands or feet. The game is over when one team hits the ball through the ring – either directly or by bouncing it off the wall – or when a requisite number of points, gained through certain types of shots, are accumulated. This is no sporting event but a contest of great religious and political significance with the opposing teams representing different religious forces.

After many attempts at hitting the ball through the rings the teams are beginning to tire in the heat of the sun. At last, the player sees his opportunity and shoots a glorious, well-angled shot from his hip. The ball glances off the wall, bounces through the ring, and the game is over. Uxmal and its gods have triumphed over the forces of Kabah and the gods of the underworld.

As leader of the winning team the player is presented with fine jewelry, including a necklace of jade beads. The teams, the ruler of Uxmal, and his family, all form a procession and the leader of the losing team is dragged forward. His playing equipment is pulled from his body roughly, and he is bound head and foot by ropes. Slumped in shame, he is carried in front of the ruler as the procession winds its way back to the main temple. There he will be decapitated by the high priest to celebrate the victory by Uxmal, and his body rolled down the long steps to the plaza floor below.

The Northern Maya Lowlands after AD 800

Various trends become apparent throughout much of the Classic Period of Maya development: increasing population; growing nucleation toward the center of many cities; craft specialization; a growth in power and wealth of the elite; expanding bureaucracies; increased social stratification; more pressure on the agricultural system; and an increase in competition and conflict between sites. All these trends caused great internal strains both on society and the environment, reaching a peak in the Southern Maya Lowlands in the late eighth-early ninth centuries AD, just when the Maya were coming under external economic and military pressure as well. New research also indicates that a lengthy drought may have begun at this time.

As a result, in the ninth century, many of the cities in the Southern Lowlands were abandoned and there was a significant depopulation of parts of the region, although the exact trigger(s) for this demise are still unclear. The traditional Classic Maya "collapse" has been used to mark the point when Maya civilization went into decline. Many

61 General view of Uxmal showing the House of the Turtles (left), the Nunnery (center), and the Temple of the Magician (right).

scholars, however, now argue that if the Maya Lowlands are examined as a whole, a different pattern begins to emerge.

Just as the southern cities were diminishing in importance, those in the Northern Lowlands, such as Uxmal, Kabah, and Sayil in the Puuc region, and Chichen Itza to the northeast of the Puuc hills in the central part of Yucatan, were beginning their florescence. Some of the Puuc region sites have already been discussed. The famous city of Chichen Itza is a very large site that has never been fully mapped; therefore, its overall extent and density of occupation (and thus its inferred population) unfortunately remains unknown, although on-going research should correct this situation. On the other hand, the core of the site has been well explored, and many of its well-known buildings including the great ball court, the Central Pyramid (Castillo), the Temple of the Warriors, the Observatory (Caracol), and the Church (Iglesia) have been restored. In addition, the Sacred Well (Cenote) has been dredged and many artifacts of jade, gold, and pottery, as well

Uxmal architecture

62 (*left*) The House of the Turtles, built out of lime concrete veneered with thin stone slabs. The plain façade has three doorways, above which is a columned frieze. A row of small turtles line the upper façade.

63 (*above*) Part of the Nunnery prior to its reconstruction.

64 (*right*) Detail of part of the stone mosaic on the façade of the Palace of the Governor.

Puuc cities

65 (*above*) The arch at Labna (right) serves as a communicating doorway between two ceremonial patios. Note the representation of a thatched-roof hut on the upper façade. See also ills. 114, 116, 117.

66 (*left*) Detail of the west angle of the palace façade at Labna.

67 (*right*) The Puuc site of Xlapak is located between Sayil and Labna. The building shown here is in purest Puuc style, a cornice with short columns separating the decorated area above from the plain surface below.

as perishable wood and cloth, have been recovered. The Cenote was a pilgrimage shrine for the Maya and retained its importance even after the decline of Chichen Itza.

On the basis of architectural and stylistic similarities it used to be thought that Chichen Itza had two distinct phases of occupation, a Maya phase succeeded by a Toltec one. Recent studies of Chichen Itza, however, have raised the strong possibility that the site was never conquered by the Toltecs of Central Mexico, but rather was Maya throughout its sequence with significant contacts between the local Maya and the Chontal Maya (sometimes called the Putun) from the Gulf Coast Lowlands, who traded widely with Oaxaca and Central Mexico, as well as with Yucatan and as far south as Honduras, and whose expansion by AD 800 put military and commercial pressure on some Southern Lowland cities just prior to their decline. New research at the coastal site of Isla Cerritos to the north of Chichen Itza (by Anthony Andrews and his colleagues) has indicated that Isla Cerritos probably was Chichen Itza's port and initial point of contact with long-distance traders.

These Terminal Classic northern cities show marked continuities with their Late Classic predecessors in the south in architecture, artifacts (both stone and ceramic), religious symbolism, hieroglyphic writing, use of space, and settlement patterns. However, non-Classic Maya traits can be seen in specific art and architectural motifs including veneer masonry, mosaic façades, new stylistic themes – rattlesnake, death, and militaristic – and special kinds of mass-produced ceramics, some of which were introduced by the Chontal Maya. In other words, by the beginning of the ninth century AD, there was a major shift in demography, as well as in political and economic power, from the south to the north. This shift, which may have been caused in part by changing economic patterns throughout ancient Mexico, did not really constitute a significant break in the development of the Maya, as Uxmal or Chichen Itza are as "Classic" as Tikal and Palenque.

The construction of Uxmal, it can be claimed, represented the peak achievement in Maya site planning. As the architect George Andrews has perceptively stated: "At Uxmal the Mayas succeeded in creating a truly monumental architecture – that completely denies its dependence on nature by its insistence on conforming to abstract rules of order and form as determined by man."[9]

The transition from Terminal Classic to Postclassic Periods falls

68 Mayapan's ruined pyramid is a smaller version of the Castillo at Chichen Itza.

between AD 900 and 1200 with the collapse first of the Puuc sites and then of Chichen Itza. The reasons for the decline of these sites remain unclear although political in-fighting, ecological problems, and the economic and political consequences of the fall of Tula in Central Mexico, are among the factors that have been suggested, with the first two the more likely. The subsequent rise of the city of Mayapan marks the beginning of a new period of Maya development that lasts until the Spanish Conquest in the early sixteenth century. Mayapan moved into the political and economic vacuum created by the demise of the earlier sites and replaced Chichen Itza as the dominant site in the northern Maya world. In fact, its central precinct has many resemblances to that of Chichen Itza with a pyramid that is a smaller version of the Castillo.

Why Mayapan is located where it is also is an unresolved question, since the agricultural potential of the land around the city is relatively poor. However, it is centrally located in Northern Yucatan – perhaps another example of the "disembedded capital" (see Chapter Three) – and has a number of natural wells for the easy acquisition of water in an environment lacking in rivers and lakes. Mayapan was a densely settled walled city with a population at its height of about 12,000 people, the center of a confederacy that controlled Northern Yucatan. It boasted few large public buildings and there was a definite decline in

Chichen Itza's Sacred Well

69–71 The Sacred Well, or Cenote of Sacrifice (*below*), was a venerated place into which offerings of jade, gold, obsidian, and wood, as well as occasional human sacrifices, were thrown. Dredging operations at the beginning of the century, and more recently scuba diving, have brought numerous finds to light, such as a gold disk depicting warriors (*left*). The gold was probably imported from lower Central America. The reconstruction drawing (*right*) shows the relationship of the Cenote to the main plaza of Chichen Itza dominated by the Castillo. To the right is the great ball court while to the left lies the Court of the Thousand Columns.

Chichen Itza architecture

72 (*above*) The impressive Castillo is the tallest structure at the site.

73 (*left*) A *chacmool* figure and rattlesnake columns stare out from the top of the Temple of the Warriors. Reclining figures such as this are thought to be connected with sacrifices. Compare ill. 82.

74 (*right*) Serpent columns on the Temple of the Jaguars flank the entrance to the building. The heads of the reptiles rest on the temple platform. Their bodies form the columns themselves, and their tails support the architecture.

artistic standards compared with earlier times. Some scholars studying the art and architecture of this time have labeled it the "Decadent" period. This impression is arguable, however, since new developments in political and economic organization were also undertaken. Complex, long-distance trading networks were set up enabling the movement by waterborne transport of bulk goods such as salt, cacao, cotton, honey, and ceramics, and lithic materials such as obsidian, which recent research on the important trading center of Cozumel Island, as well as ethnohistoric documentation, has helped to confirm. Religion, while as important as ever, appears to have become more decentralized than in the Classic Period. Thus, this period does not appear to be culturally "decadent."

Mayapan and its confederacy fell from power in the mid-fifteenth century, and by the time the conquistadors arrived, the Maya world was lacking any centralized authority. With the coming of the Spanish, many of the elite aspects of Maya culture were destroyed. As in Central Mexico, the introduction of diseases against which the Maya had no immunity played a major part in the decline of the population. The Spanish, however, had great difficulty in totally eliminating Maya political and military resistance, which continued for several centuries.

In sum, it has become increasingly clear that although certain aspects of Maya development differ from those of other Mesoamerican groups, many of the general trends are quite similar. Far from being unique, the Maya were an integral and closely related part of the ancient Mexican civilizational system. Moreover, their history was not as homogeneous as previously thought but was replete with many rises and falls, significant economic and political competition, and shifts in power.

CHAPTER SEVEN

Tula: Capital of Toltec Mexico

After Teotihuacan's decline in the mid-eighth century AD, there followed a time of political and economic fragmentation, competition, and change, as various groups throughout Mesoamerica sought to fill the vacuum created by that great city's demise. One of the centers that emerged as a major focus of political and economic influence was Tula (or the legendary city of Tollan), capital of the Toltecs. Although smaller and less planned than Teotihuacan, Tula served as the center for the expansive Toltec military might and had trading contacts with groups throughout ancient Mexico and even into Central America.

TIME: AD 1000

PLACE: Tula, north of the Valley of Mexico in the modern state of Hidalgo

CIVILIZATION: Toltec

The child puts on her heavy cotton shirt to keep out the cold and leaves her house. It may be early, but the courtyard is already full of cooking smells and the sound of people moving about. The child stops to watch several artisans laying out their tools. Some weavers are spinning cotton yarn; one is making a simple cloak, while another is working hard on a headband for a feather headdress. The child picks up a broken spindle whorl and runs her fingers over the elaborate incised pattern of triangles.

In the next courtyard several women sit in the shade on one side of the open plaza, painting decorations on ceramic bowls. Quite a variety of different pot types are available in the city, but imported ones with a lustrous finish are the most coveted. Wealthy people, in particular, own these pots. Some are quite standard shapes while others are molded into different animal forms. One that is displayed during ceremonies at the local shrine is an eagle with the head of a warrior emerging from its mouth.

Several other potters are working nearby, using clay molds to make small ceramic figurines. Each mold is a different human or animal shape. The child's family owns several such figurines including a bird that is used as a ritual object within the home.

To an outsider the city's zig-zagging paths appear haphazard, but the residents have no difficulty in following them. The child heads along one of them toward the district that houses the elite and the priests. She passes another group of craftspeople making large stone bowls. These can only be for the rich, for she has never seen such bowls in her own neighborhood. The work is slow and laborious. One artisan draws a piece of rope back and forth through a groove as he cuts a large block of stone in half. Tired of watching, the child wanders on.

Now the path becomes wider and well paved. She passes a wall with a parapet of carved stone skulls. She is nearing the most sacred part of the city where human sacrifices are made to terrifying gods. A little further on the path opens onto a huge plaza surrounded by some of the largest and most impressive structures in the city.

The child stays near the corner of one of the buildings. Although no one has ever forbidden her to enter the plaza, she knows she should probably not be there. In the next plaza, that is paved and plastered, all the ceremonies in honor of the most sacred gods, such as Quetzalcoatl, the "feathered serpent" and "morning star," are held. The great warriors of Tula, pride of the city, are practicing their stances. Favored by the gods, they have made the city renowned the world over. They are dressed in cotton uniform and some wear headdresses. Each carries an elaborately decorated shield with either jaguar or eagle designs. Some wield large clubs, while others hone their skills with dart-throwers. These throwers are made of wood and provide artificial extensions of the warriors' arms. The darts can then be hurled a greater distance and with more power than can be achieved by an arm and hand throw alone.

Suddenly, one warrior calls out to the others. They gather round as another Toltec warrior steps forward and confronts a foreign soldier captured in a recent battle. Each warrior is given a large wooden club embedded with sharp obsidian chips and they begin to fight. This is no mock battle. The captive is soon covered in blood from the blows and numerous cuts he receives, and the Toltec raises his arms in triumph. The defeated warrior is carried off to a nearby platform crowned by an altar shaped like a reclining deity. He is seized by a group of priests, laid back on the statue, and sacrificed. This is the harsh reality of life at Tula. The gods demand blood, and the Toltecs must appease them.

75 Roll-out drawing of the carvings on a square shaft roof support from the summit of Pyramid B at Tula. Tied bundles of spears or darts can be seen between armed Toltec warriors.

Central Mexico: The Toltecs

The Toltecs are one of the most well-known peoples in Precolumbian archaeology, and their military prowess and ruthlessness were featured widely in many popular accounts of ancient Mexico. Such fame is in part due to the heroic deeds ascribed to the Toltecs by their successors, the Aztecs, whose history was in turn recorded and transmitted to the Western world by the Spaniards. The Aztecs wished to promote their own importance by linking themselves with the "glory" of the Toltecs whose supposed achievements reached mythical proportions in the Aztecs' rewritten version of history. By the time the Spaniards recorded various historical/legendary information about the Toltecs, more than four centuries had elapsed since their fall from power, which means that the historical data from the sixteenth century available about the Toltecs must be approached with great caution. It

76 Pyramid B at Tula, with the Vestibule and the Burned Palace in the foreground.

is likely that their achievements were not nearly as great as was originally believed.

The nature of the Toltec people and their accomplishments remain, therefore, enigmatic, despite all their celebrity. Their capital city of Tula, for example, was not identified archaeologically until the pathbreaking research of Wigberto Jimenez Moreno and Jorge Acosta in the 1940s. Even though important new archaeological research at Tula, Hidalgo, has improved our understanding of the Toltecs, much still remains to be done.

Recent research at Tula by archaeologists Richard Diehl, Eduardo Matos Moctezuma, and their colleagues, indicates that the Toltecs became a force to be reckoned with by AD 900. They may have originated in western and northern Mexico, living on the peripheries of

Tula architecture

77 (*above left*) The carved wall or Coatepantli behind Pyramid B depicts feathered rattlesnakes – one of the god Quetzalcoatl's guises – eating human skeletons.

78 (*left*) Pyramid C, which has been only partially reconstructed.

79 (*above*) Detail from the wall of Pyramid B of an eagle eating a human heart.

the civilizational system and probably being forced to move south because of deteriorating climatic conditions in their homelands. After settling at Tula their economic and political importance began to increase. Like the Teotihuacanos, whom we met in Chapter Four, their strength was based, in part, on their control of significant obsidian deposits, particularly the highly prized green obsidian from Pachuca. It was probably furthered by the extension of their economic power through military coercion and conquest, although the archaeological evidence for this is far from clear.

At Tula, the eminence of the military in the Toltec world is reflected in the prominent positions accorded the symbols of the military orders of the jaguars and eagles. Death and blood also figured prominently in Toltec symbolism, as is reflected in the carved skull racks and depictions of eagles eating hearts that can be found at the site. The Toltecs' military prowess is further revealed in the legends that the Spaniards recorded some centuries later, but we should remain aware that their militarism may be exaggerated here.

The heyday of Tula and the Toltecs was relatively shortlived, lasting from AD 900 to 1100, at the latest. Research recently conducted at Tula indicates that the site did not begin to rise to prominence until at least AD 800, after the fall of Teotihuacan, and that it was probably not involved in the latter event. Tula may have benefited from Teotihuacan's demise, however, since analyses of ceramics and artifacts at Tula suggest that at least part of its rapid population increase was caused by the resettlement of refugees from the Teotihuacan Valley, as well as by immigrants from north and west Mexico.

Tula never reached the size of Teotihuacan. Its maximum population was probably somewhere between 35,000 and 60,000 people, according to Diehl, and its area never exceeded 14 square kilometers. Moreover, the settlement of the city does not appear to have been highly organized, particularly when compared with the great degree of urban planning at Teotihuacan.

Toltec religion is a fascinating area of study because the rich ethnohistoric accounts from the sixteenth century can be used to illuminate archaeological materials directly. Two of the deities who held a prominent place in the Toltec pantheon were Quetzalcoatl, the "feathered serpent" and "morning star," and Tezcatlipoca, the god of war. A reclining sculptured figure with an offering plate on its stomach, known as a *chacmool*, is also found at Tula and at sites directly or

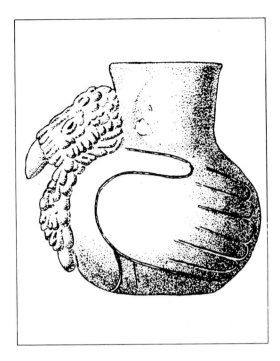

80 A ceramic jar, a turkey effigy, with a lead-like finish known as Plumbate. This pottery was made on the Pacific side of the northern Guatemalan Highlands and found in some quantity at Tula.

indirectly in contact with the Toltecs, such as Chichen Itza. It has been speculated that the plate was to hold hearts when first removed from sacrificial victims.

Toltec influence – certainly economic and perhaps political – can be seen throughout West Mexico and may be partly responsible for drawing this region fully into the orbit of the civilizational system of ancient Mexico. Toltec influence also reached south into both the Northern Maya Lowlands and the Guatemalan Highlands where contemporaneous and later-ruling lineages wanted to link themselves with Toltec ancestors. Large quantities of a type of pottery known as Tohil Plumbate were imported to Tula from a region adjacent to this highland zone.

As well as having contacts with the Lowland Maya as we saw at the site of Chichen Itza in the last chapter, the Toltecs also had close economic relations to the east with central and northern Gulf Coast groups, and they conducted exchanges to the south with Oaxaca and Tlaxcala, especially with the site of Cholula, which is reflected in the movement of distinctively painted pottery vessels in the period AD 900 to 1100. Toltec contacts also went well beyond the borders of ancient

Toltec warriors

81 (*left*) Early Postclassic stela from Tula showing a warrior with a Tlaloc-and-year sign headdress.

82 (*below*) A *chacmool* from in front of Pyramid B at Tula. The figure wears a sacrificial knife strapped to the left arm. Compare ill. 73.

83 (*right*) These huge Atlantean warriors helped support the roof of the temple crowning Pyramid B at Tula.

Mexico, both to the south as far as Costa Rica – as shown by some of the ceramic finds at Tula – and to the north, as far as the American Southwest – as some archaeologists have hypothesized on the basis of trade goods, such as copper bells and macaws, that apparently moved between the northern fringes of Mesoamerica and the Southwest. Although there certainly was some trade between Central Mexico and the Southwest, the strength, directness, and dating of these contacts, as well as the putative role of the Toltecs, are still a matter of considerable debate in the archaeological literature.

The reasons for the disintegration of Toltec power and influence remain totally unclear, although Tula continued to be occupied into Aztec times, well after its extra-regional importance had vanished.

CHAPTER EIGHT

The Aztecs and Tenochtitlan

The last great urban center to emerge in ancient Mexico was Tenochtitlan, capital of the Aztec empire. This city was founded in AD 1325 on an island near the western shores of a swampy lake in the Valley of Mexico. Over the next 194 years, up to the time of Cortés and his soldiers, the Aztecs built from nothing an urban center that grew into a metropolis housing perhaps as many as 200,000 people. Such a large population, which provided labor to build the awe-inspiring structures like the huge Templo Mayor (or Great Temple) in the heart of the city and the large causeways that linked the city with the mainland, was in part made possible by the intensive agricultural system that the Aztecs developed. The Aztecs in effect combined the highly nucleated and planned urban design of the Teotihuacanos and the militaristically oriented expansion of the Toltecs to produce, by the dawn of the sixteenth century, their great imperial capital of Tenochtitlan.

TIME: AD 1500

PLACE: Tenochtitlan, Valley of Mexico

CIVILIZATION: Aztec (Mexica)

The farmer stands waist deep in the muddy water of the canal cutting large leafy weeds and throwing them onto a wooden raft. When he has a sufficient load, he will tow the raft to the small rectangular plots of land (*chinampas*) that he cultivates along the canal. A number of his neighbors – many of them his relatives – undertake similar tasks, such as scooping the thick mud from the canal and throwing it onto their fields. With sides held together by wooden stakes and branches, the garden-sized plots look rather like small islands.

Although it is back-breaking work and the stench from the canal is overwhelming, the farmer knows he has somehow to maintain the plots, whatever the cost. Artificially built up from canal silt and marsh weeds, the *chinampas* can all too easily revert to their former status as swamp land. Their fertility depends on irrigation from the canals and the regular application of human manure, collected in small barges from the great city of Tenochtitlan just a short way to the north. All the farmer's labors, and those of thousands of *chinampa*-farmers like him, are devoted to the production of crops and other plants for the citizens of Tenochtitlan. Generations of Aztecs have toiled to create this magnificent island city and the hugely productive land around it, and the farmer knows that it would be more than his life is worth to neglect his duties now.

The farmer had always taken his *chinampa* fields for granted until he attended a cousin's wedding in the distant mountains to the west. He saw how dependent they were there on good rainfall and how they could grow only one maize crop a year. Moreover, they were unable to use the same field year after year but had to shift their cultivation regularly to let the soil lie fallow and become fertile again. Even some of their neighbors, who were able to irrigate their fields with water from an adjacent stream, were still limited to two crops a year.

The farmer's *chinampas* can be used year after year, and he is usually able to obtain at least two different yields annually of a variety of crops such as maize, squashes and beans. He also grows flowers that are in great demand in the marketplace. The flexibility of the plots is such that he is able to reserve corners as nurseries where seedlings can be grown and then replanted throughout the plots.

The farmer wants to complete his task quickly so that he and his wife can visit the great market in the Tlatelolco district of Tenochtitlan the next day. There will not be time later as the head of his clan has asked him to help repair an earthen dike near a new area of *chinampa* plots that other members of his clan have recently built.

Next morning the farmer and his wife prepare for their trip and step down from their house, which is raised off the marshy shoreline on low wooden stilts. Sometimes when they travel to Tenochtitlan they load their canoe and paddle north to the city, but since they are only taking flowers they decide to walk. Carefully wrapping the plants to preserve their freshness, and placing them in large sacks which they carry on their backs, they set off. With a major festival taking place in the capital in the next few days, their flowers will sell quickly.

The well-maintained causeway is crowded with travelers even in the early morning hours. Although it would be simpler to stop on the roadside and sell to passers by, they resist the temptation as they have had grim warnings of the gods' strict injunctions against selling outside the market.

Soon, in the distance, they can see the huge twin temples that crown the great pyramid near the intersection of the main north, south, and west causeways. The market is just beyond. They pass the sacred precinct where the emperor lives, and avoid a series of houses belonging to the nobility that are much grander than the modest ones with which they are familiar. At last they reach the market of Tlatelolco, once a separate city but now absorbed into the expanding metropolis of Tenochtitlan.

The flower sellers are all in one section of the market. The farmer and his wife sit down to join them, spreading their flowers out on a cloth. They have a successful day, and at the end of it are able to buy a pointed wooden digging stick in another part of the market where tools are sold, before setting off for home.

84 A model of part of the market at Tlatelolco. Vendors sit on the ground and spread their wares on cloths before them.

Central Mexico: The Aztecs

With the rise of the Aztecs in the two centuries prior to the Spanish Conquest of 1521 we leave the realm of legend and enter that of fully recorded history. For the first time, scholars have more historical data available than archaeological information. Aztec achievements were outstanding, in particular their urban accomplishments at Tenochtitlan. The early Spanish sources often do not know which superlatives to use to inform their readers about what they saw. Bernal Díaz del Castillo has written that when the conquistadors first saw Tenochtitlan, the capital city of the Aztec state, they wondered "if this was real that we saw before our eyes."[10] Cortés, himself, in a letter to the Emperor Charles V of Spain, tells the emperor that he "will describe some of those [things] I have seen which . . . will . . . be so remarkable as not to be believed, for we who saw them with our own eyes could not grasp them with understanding."[11]

85 Excavations in the heart of Mexico City have revealed the remains of the Great Temple (*Templo Mayor*) of Tenochtitlan. These standard-bearer sculptures were found reclining against the stairway of the Stage III Temple leading to the shrine of the war god, Huitzilopochtli.

The Aztecs are one of the most incredible success stories in ancient Mexico. In the aftermath of the decline of Tula, a political free-for-all ensued in Central Mexico. Emigrating Toltecs from Tula moved south into the Basin, as did other groups from the north and west. A variety of city-states became scattered throughout the Basin – some new, others with older roots – competing with one another for power. The last people to enter the Basin, the Aztecs, arrived from somewhere to the northwest probably during the thirteenth century. This small group found the most acceptable sites in the Basin already occupied, and so they went to work for one of the established cities.[12]

The Aztecs' most saleable skill was their military ability. They therefore served as mercenaries for the large city-state of Colhuacan. But their "uncivilized" ways were their undoing, one event in particular: as a reward for their loyalty and prowess, their employer

The city of Tenochtitlan

86 (*left*) Head of the monumental stone relief of the goddess Coyolxauhqui found at the foot of the Great Temple stairway in 1978. The discovery of this relief renewed interest in the remains of the Aztec sacred center.

87 (*below*) A model (made before the recent excavations) of the huge ceremonial precinct at the heart of Tenochtitlan. The Great Temple in the center background dominates the enclosure.

88 (*right*) Drawing of the Great Temple with its skull-rack altar, or *tzompantli*, from a sixteenth-century codex. Heads of sacrificial victims may have been placed on the altar during certain ceremonies.

Templo del ydolo Vitzilo
puestli.

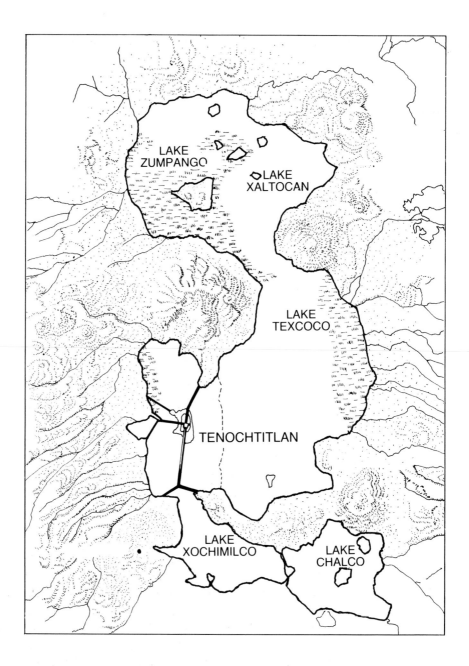

89 The Valley of Mexico showing the location of Tenochtitlan on an island in Lake Texcoco. Three causeways lead to the north, south, and west.

offered the hand of a royal princess in marriage to the leader of the Aztecs, but instead of a marriage ceremony the Aztecs flayed the woman and used her skin in one of their rituals. As a consequence the Aztecs were banished in AD 1325 (or 1345 according to a different reading of the historical sources by some authorities) to the swampy shores of Lake Texcoco, one of the several lakes that covered much of the Basin of Mexico in Precolumbian times (nearly all of these lakes were subsequently drained by the Spanish). For most peoples, this event would have been the end of the road. But such were the capabilities and determination of the Aztecs that they seized the opportunities presented by their new, highly unpromising surroundings and in a relatively brief period of time began to reclaim the swamp land and build up the two adjacent, off-shore islands of Tenochtitlan and Tlatelolco.

The Aztecs did not just reclaim swamp land. They constructed agricultural plots on this reclaimed land; piped water from one zone to another; and built an immense dike to keep the salt water from eastern and northern parts of the lake system from ruining the agriculturally suitable fresh water of the west and south. As Michael D. Coe has stated, this entire zone "represented a gigantic hydraulic scheme based on land drainage and the manipulation of water resources."[13]

Over the following decades, through both a series of astute political alliances and skilled fighting, the Aztecs increased their power and influence. By 1428, under their talented new emperor Itzcoatl (1427–1440), the Aztecs defeated their last remaining adversary and emerged as the dominant force in the Basin of Mexico. In the succeeding years, under a series of emperors, particularly Ahuitzotl (1486–1502), the Aztecs not only consolidated their power in Central Mexico but began to spread their influence to the farther reaches of Mesoamerica as shown by the map on page 128.

For the first time, we have definite evidence for a political empire in ancient Mexico, controlled by the Aztecs from their great city of Tenochtitlan. Tribute lists from the time of the Conquest provide information about the huge flow of goods, such as cotton clothes, feathers, and vast amounts of various foodstuffs, which arrived in Tenochtitlan from the conquered territories. Organized merchant groups spread Aztec economic influence even further and also acted for the state as agents and spies.

The capital city, which may have had a population as high as 200,000 to 300,000 in the early sixteenth century, was a superb example of

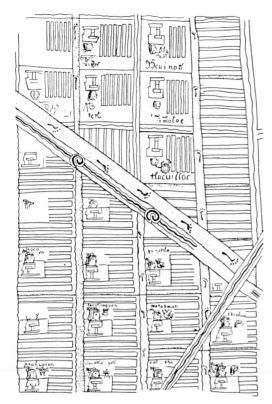

Chinampa farmers

Much of the Aztecs' success rested on their ability to reclaim swampland and to build *chinampas*, or artificial fields, for cultivation.

90 (*left*) A sixteenth-century plan of a *chinampa* zone near Tenochtitlan.

91 (*below left*) Modern-day *chinampa* near Mexico City.

92 (*below*) Schematic cross-section of a *chinampa* showing how the Aztecs built up land from weeds and mud and held it together by inserting stakes and planting willow trees.

93 (*right*) Drawings from Fray Sahagún's sixteenth-century *History of the Things of New Spain* show an Aztec using a digging stick both to sow seeds and harvest the crop, as well as taking produce to market.

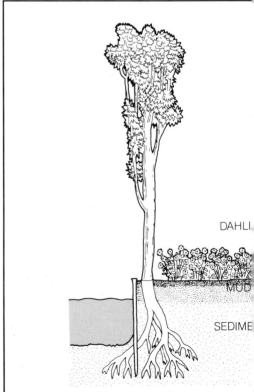

DAHLI.

MUD

SEDIME

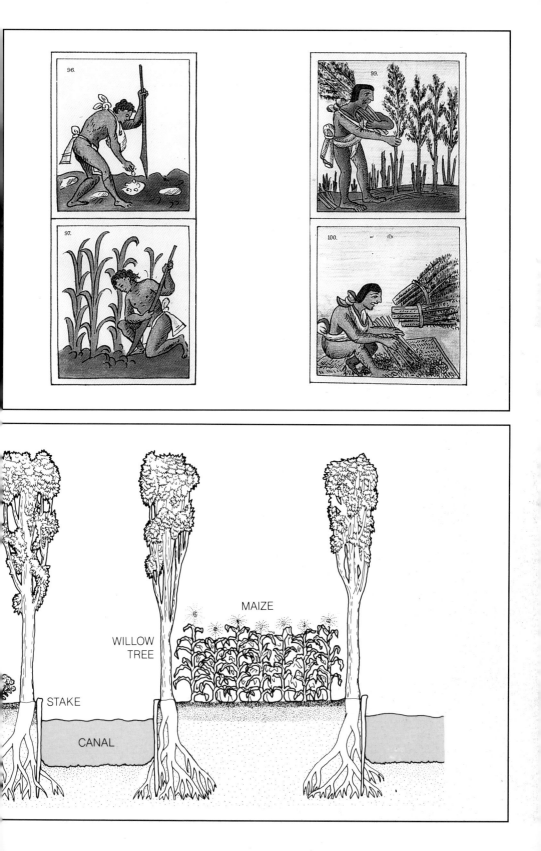

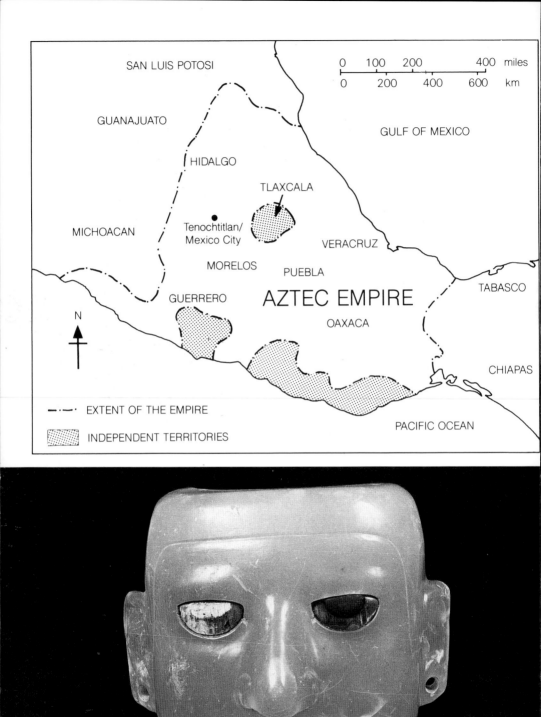

The riches of Aztec civilization

The Aztecs traded widely, bringing precious goods to Tenochtitlan from all corners of their empire.

4 (*above left*) The extent of the empire in AD 1519, the year of Cortés's arrival in Mexico.

5 (*left*) Alabaster mask found in the Great Temple excavations.

6 (*above*) The emperor Moctezuma's headdress, made mainly of green quetzal feathers, was given to Cortés as a gift for his sovereign. Remarkably it survives to this day and can be seen in Vienna, Austria.

7 (*right*) A stone mask representing the Aztec deity Xipe Totec, the flayed god associated with planting and springtime.

planned growth. By building out into the lake, the Aztecs consolidated and enlarged the original two islands which in turn were linked to the mainland by three large causeways. Fresh water was brought to the city from the mainland by aqueduct.

By 1502, when Moctezuma II (or Motecuhzoma Xocoyotzin to give him his accurately transliterated name) ascended the throne, the Aztec empire had become the most powerful state in the history of ancient Mexico. But for all its wealth and influence, it was a fragile empire. Many aspects of Aztec culture were still in flux or beginning to change when Cortés and his conquistadors arrived just seventeen years later. Enlisting the crucial aid of rival states such as Tlaxcala, which the Aztecs had failed to conquer despite its close proximity to Tenochtitlan, Cortés exploited this vulnerability with considerable skill. Utilizing his technological superiority and the large-scale support of his new allies, as well as exploiting the debilitation of the Aztecs resulting from the devastating epidemic in Tenochtitlan that occurred in 1520, in less than two years Cortés was able to defeat the Aztecs. By 1521, Moctezuma was already dead (having been killed the previous year), Tenochtitlan was in ruins, and the centralized Aztec state was demolished.

In the years that followed, the destruction that Cortés visited upon the Aztec world was completed by infectious diseases. Measles and smallpox wreaked havoc upon Central Mexico and on populations throughout the New World that had no natural immunities against these Old World killer illnesses. One of the worst demographic tragedies in human history ensued with millions of native Americans losing their lives in the subsequent fifty years. The complex, civilized world of ancient Mexico, which had produced such marvels as Teotihuacan and Tenochtitlan over a 3,000-year-long period, came to an abrupt, catastrophic end.

PART II

What were their origins?

CHAPTER NINE

The Roots of
Mexican Civilization

We have seen that ancient Mexico from about 1200 BC to the time of the Spanish Conquest was home to a series of complex civilizations, all of which had economic, political, and religious connections. But was this complex system "home-grown," or was it introduced from outside Mexico?

Ever since the Precolumbian civilizations of the New World became known to the Western world there has been much speculation about their origins. The great pyramids at Teotihuacan, or the lowland Maya pyramids, immediately called the attention of some observers to the similarities between such structures and the pyramids of Egypt. Others remarked on the apparent stylistic similarities between features of Maya art and various artistic styles among the ancient civilizations of the Old World. Still others noted the "Negroid" appearance of the great Olmec stone heads and compared them with the features of the inhabitants of West Africa.

Despite relatively scant encouragement from professional archaeologists, these kinds of comparisons and attendant hypotheses about origins were not just eighteenth- or nineteenth-century phenomena but have continued to flourish to the present day. In fact, a few recent efforts, such as those as Von Däniken, have taken on a distinctly modern twist with claims made for the presence of depictions of ancient astronauts from outer space on Maya sculpture.

All of these efforts have one thing in common: they see the source of certain aspects, or the entirety, of ancient Mexican civilization as lying beyond the frontiers of the Mesoamerican world. These "external" origin hypotheses are opposed to "internal" ones that view the development of Mexican civilization as untouched by outside influences. In certain instances, the external hypotheses argue for the importation of specific traits, while in others they argue for more general external influences on the growth of ancient Mexican civilization.

In some cases, the external hypotheses seem to operate from the premise that the indigenous Mexican cultures were not capable of inventing a certain trait, and therefore it must have been brought in from some foreign land. Such views suffer from an implicit racism of which the writers may well be unaware. The reasons why the local culture could not invent the trait are never adequately discussed. Clearly, it is felt that Mexican civilization was too "primitive." These kinds of arguments fail to take into account the complexity, sophistication, and long-term (approximately 3,000 years) growth trends of Mexican civilization.

In other cases, the external hypotheses are based on the strong conviction that the similarities in traits between Mexico and another place are simply too close to have been coincidental, and that there must have been contacts. Scholars who have advanced these arguments believe that independent invention of cultural traits is unlikely. It is interesting to note that in virtually every one of these hypotheses cultural influence is seen as coming to Mexico, and not the other way around.

Let us examine several examples that attempt to illustrate external influences on Mexico. Some arguments, although very popular, are difficult to take seriously because of the sheer lack of evidence to support them or because of their incompleteness. For instance, claims that relate developments in Mexico to incursions from peoples from "Atlantis" or "Mu" must be dismissed as total fantasy until such time as the mysterious island in the Atlantic/Pacific which is invoked as the source of the "influences" can positively be identified, its culture described, and specific links between the island and Mexico established. To reply that such requirements cannot be met because the island has disappeared under the sea is clearly inadequate. When claims are made for the importance of a place, the burden of proof is on the claimants to offer at least some *positive* evidence in substantiation of their arguments.

Theories, such as those of Peter Tompkins in his book *Mysteries of the Mexican Pyramids*, that link the pyramids of Egypt and Mexico, also find no support in the available archaeological data. In fact, the last of the great pyramids at Giza on the Nile were built nearly 3,000 years before the great pyramids of the Sun and Moon at Teotihuacan, or the well-known pyramids in the Maya Lowlands. As Kurt Mendels-

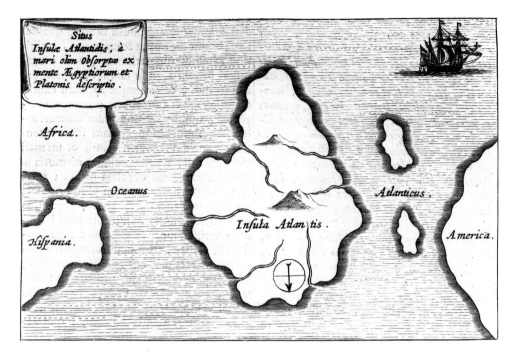

98 A fanciful seventeenth-century map (with north to the bottom) showing the supposed location of the island of Atlantis.

sohn has pointed out, it is difficult to imagine a boatload of ancient Egyptians arriving in Mexico and introducing a monumental activity that had not been practiced in their homeland for millennia. Moreover, as many writers have argued, it is much more likely that a boatload of foreigners with no nearby support and no clear military or technological advantage would be killed before they got far from the beach rather than that they would be able to introduce a new architectural style all over ancient Mexico. In addition, the structures have major functional differences: the Egyptian pyramids come to a point and serve as tombs, while the Mexican ones are truncated and serve as foundations for temples, although they sometimes housed tombs as well.

Spectacular voyages in traditional seagoing vessels, such as the well-known scholar-adventurer Thor Heyerdahl's expedition across the Atlantic in the *Ra*, a boat made in Africa with the materials and techniques used in the past, do show that it would have been possible for ancient Egyptians to cross the ocean to Mexico. They, of course, do *not* show that these kinds of voyages did take place or what effects they might have had if they did. Would such voyages have had a significant impact on the development of ancient Mexican civilization? And if so, how? No author has yet satisfactorily demonstrated which of the

Pyramids of Mexico and Egypt

Apart from superficial similarities in shape, nothing has been discovered to connect the pyramids of the New and Old Worlds. The Egyptian monuments functioned solely as tombs for the pharaohs. Mexican pyramids, built 3,000 years after their Egyptian counterparts, were truncated and crowned by temples; only some contained tombs.

99 (*right*) Temple I at the Classic Maya site of Tikal.

100 (*below*) The Great Pyramid of Khufu (Cheops) at Giza in Egypt. A boat pit, part of the funerary complex, can be seen in the foreground.

101 (*below right*) Pyramid of the Sun at Teotihuacan.

putatively introduced innovations from Egypt would have changed the nature of culture in Mexico. Perhaps an innovation such as metal weapons? It seems not, as there were none in Mexico before the Spanish. More importantly, would the foreigners be able to impress their innovations on the Mexican populace? A simple "Take me to your leader" surely would not be successful, and, even if it was, why would the Mexican elite readily adopt what the foreigners told them or showed them? They could do it if they conquered the Mexicans, had obvious technological superiority, or were backed by external force, but there is no evidence for such conditions until the Spanish conquest in the sixteenth century AD.

Much more sophisticated and convincing arguments about *how* and *why* innovations would have been accepted, and *what* their long-term effects might have been, are needed if the external-influence hypotheses are to play a more serious role in scholarly discussions. Pointing to similarities in objects, styles, or other cultural practices is, on its own, insufficient. One has only to look to the historical record to see how similarities (which have sometimes been labeled "parallel evolution") have developed between very separate cultures; compare, for example, the feudal systems of Europe and Japan, or the rise of agriculture in different parts of the world, or the invention of pottery many times over. Thus, while Heyerdahl's book and movie rightfully impress the public with their tales of heroism and adventure, they have had little impact on the continuing debate about external influences on the development of ancient Mexican civilization.

The newest, space-age version of the outlandish arguments for external influences, and perhaps the most popular – if one uses the guideline of the number of books sold, or the number of times movies are repeated on television – is Erich Von Däniken's speculations on the importance of visits to earth from denizens of outer space. Many years ago, I appeared on a television talk program with Von Däniken and also had a chance to chat with him after the show. After discussing the problems with his interpretations of the carving on top of the great sarcophagus of Pacal found beneath the Temple of the Inscriptions (see Chapter Five) at the Maya site of Palenque – Von Däniken argued that the sculpture depicted an ancient astronaut taking off at the controls of a space ship while I contended that it actually showed a Maya *falling*, not rising, into the underworld – I pointed out the potentially racist implications of what he was saying. In particular, I stressed that, in the Maya case, what he in effect was stating was that

Voyagers from overseas?

102,103 Was ancient Mexican civilization brought by foreigners from far-distant places? There is no evidence for the idea. Thor Heyerdahl's brave voyage across the Atlantic Ocean in his replica reed boat, Ra II (*above*), proves only that the ancient Egyptians could have crossed to the Americas, not that they did. Thanks to recent excavations in Newfoundland, Canada, we now know that the Vikings landed there in their longships (*below*) by the eleventh century AD, but Canada is a long way from Mexico and we have no evidence that the Vikings traveled farther south.

Visitors from outer space?

104,105 Erich Von Däniken has speculated
that the sarcophagus lid of the ruler Pacal
(*right*), found beneath the Temple of the
Inscriptions at Palenque, depicts an ancient
astronaut at the controls of a space ship. He
bases this idea on the apparently similar
position of modern astronauts in a flight
capsule, like the crew of the Apollo 12
(*above*). Was civilization therefore
introduced to Mexico by aliens from
another planet? Unfortunately for Von
Däniken, there is consistent iconographic
evidence to indicate that Pacal is not being
pushed back by gravity as he takes off but
is descending into the underworld. Von
Däniken's claims find no support in the art
or archaeology of ancient Mexico.

African contacts?

106,107 Superficially at least there are facial similarities between this Olmec colossal head from La Venta (*above*) and a thirteenth-century terracotta portrait of an Ife woman from Nigeria (*right*) in West Africa. Such shared "Negroid" features have led some to suggest an African origin for Olmec culture. But similar facial traits can be found among Native American populations and so far there is no archaeological evidence for any African contacts.

143

given that the Maya were not capable of inventing the complex hieroglyphic, calendrical, and mathematical systems depicted on their monuments, therefore they must have been introduced by external agents. It was curious, I remarked, that virtually all his examples of the evidence of "ancient astronauts" and their major impacts on historical developments came from either "third world" or "primitive" peoples, and not from Western civilization. The inference was clear: non-Western peoples were incapable of "advanced" developments and so needed outside help, while Western peoples were capable and did not need such aid. Why did he not offer any examples of ancient astronauts coming to aid Michelangelo in his marvelous paintings in the Sistine Chapel, for instance? His reply was totally disarming and precluded further discussion. He acknowledged the argument by saying something like "good point" and then proceeded to say that he would have to explore it in his next book! I still await such a book.

Nevertheless, the basic underestimation of the cultural capabilities of peoples such as the ancient Maya, or the lack of understanding of cultural invention, whether from bias or inadvertence, still remains. While there is no doubt that it is possible to find incongruous cultures and ideas or objects, many of the examples in the non-professional literature, like Von Däniken's, abound with misunderstandings of cultural development and are based on untenable premises that cannot be substantiated.

Not all discussions of external influences on the growth of ancient Mexican civilization can be so easily dismissed, however. Ivan Van Sertima has garnered indirect evidence which points, he believes, to the west coast of Africa as the direct source of the Olmec accomplishments. Two of his arguments include the "Negroid" appearance of the great Olmec stone heads, and the great sailing abilities of coastal African groups. The respected archaeologist Betty Meggers has also argued for the external origin of the Olmec, pointing out what she believes are a number of stylistic similarities between Olmec and Chinese art, particularly of the Shang period (*c* 1700–1100 BC). She notes, for instance, that feline figures are prominent features in both art styles. R.A. Jairazbhoy, in *Ancient Egyptians and Chinese in America*, also offers a lengthy list of similarities between the Olmec and both the Chinese and Egyptians. Up to now, however, these arguments generally relate to impressionistic comparisons of style, and not to concrete archaeological evidence of contact, and I do not find them convincing.

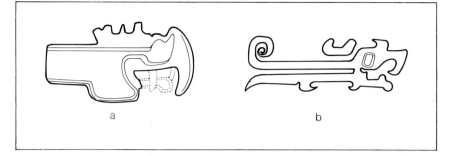

108 **Contacts with the Orient?** Similar "dragon" motifs from Costa Rica (*a*) and Shang China (*b*) are among certain symbols that have prompted some scholars to suggest a direct oriental influence in Mesoamerica. But these arguments relate only to impressionistic comparisons of style and do not form any concrete evidence for contact.

Certain basic shapes and representations such as circles, squares, and crosses, and a variety of geometric motifs, show up repeatedly in widely separated art styles, as do representations of important aspects of the environment such as prominent animals like wild cats (be they tigers or jaguars). These stylistic similarities between different cultures must be linked to archaeological evidence, such as trade goods or materials of definite foreign origin, if they are to be used as proof of contacts in antiquity. It has been possible, for instance, for archaeologists to demonstrate the origins of lithic materials such as obsidian and jade in a particular region through trace element analysis. If the proponents of "external contact" wish to strengthen their case, they should make use of the advanced technical resources now at the archaeologist's command. Moreover, isolated similarities should be linked to wider cultural contexts; it is the latter that should be closely compared rather than just similarities in the forms of objects.

All the above hypotheses, therefore, while assuredly provocative, still need much more support. In the case of the Olmec, a strong argument can be made for local development. The archaeologist David Grove, who has worked extensively on Olmec remains, has noted regarding the "Negroid" features of the stone heads: "While descriptive of the general facial features, this identification has been taken too literally by some authors, for such characteristics are common among Indian groups on the Gulf Coast and elsewhere in Mesoamerica, and are not indicative of transatlantic contacts."[14] Certain isolated physical features are not necessarily indications of any particular group. The Olmec style and iconography seen at the great Olmec centers in the Gulf Coast Lowlands "heartland" is actually reflective of a much broader symbolism that is to be found throughout the ancient Mexican world just prior to 1000 BC. Grove forcefully points out that the Olmec finds from archaeological sites in the Gulf Coast region "were not part of something which 'appeared suddenly,' nor for which origins must be sought elsewhere. The archaeological record bears witness to an indigenous evolution of the culture today called Olmec. The heartland was its birthplace."[15]

The problem of independent invention versus importation from external sources (what is termed "diffusion") is, therefore, one of the most difficult questions that professional archaeologists concerned with Mexican archaeology have to face. Most would agree that the development of Mexican civilization (up until the time of the arrival of the conquistadors in the sixteenth century AD) was not significantly influenced by outside forces. History gives us many examples, however, where the majority view in a debate has been proved to be wrong – but that has not happened, as yet, in this instance. Furthermore, many archaeologists would contend that this kind of

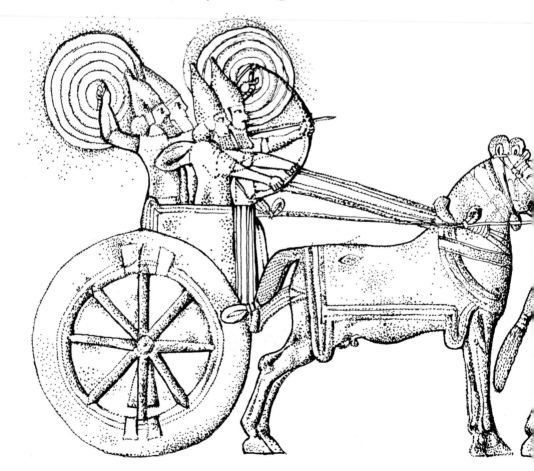

discussion totally misses the point. Even if some of the cases for long-distance diffusion could be "proven" – by, say, the finding of artifacts of definite foreign manufacture – or at least be generally accepted by a large group of scholars, such "proof" would only be the first step in a much wider analysis. Diffusionists generally devote all their energies to showing that long-distance contacts occurred, and then rest their case, instead of continuing to examine such critical questions as to *why* the trait or style was accepted and what effect it and its foreign carriers had on the indigenous culture. The probability of chance landings by boat loads of foreigners having great effects are minimal. Where such is not the case, then archaeologists need to understand why. For example, archaeological discoveries unequivocally indicate that Norsemen landed on the coast of what is now Newfoundland in Canada well before Columbus's first contact with the Americas in 1492. Yet despite the historic reality of the Norse landings, there is to date no evidence that these landfalls had any significant impact on the cultural development of the Native Americans of the area.

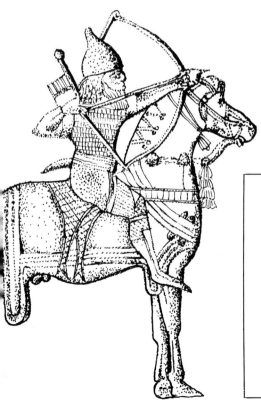

109,110 **The idea of the wheel** Today archaeologists are interested not so much in *who* first thought of an invention, but *why* it became accepted and used widely in a society. Ancient Mexicans knew of the wheel (*below*, a wheeled toy from Veracruz), but never developed vehicles like the Assyrian chariot (*left*) because they lacked the horses or other beasts of burden to pull them. In the Americas horses died out at the end of the Ice Age and were not reintroduced until the Spanish Conquest.

Archaeologists also point to examples through time where knowledge of a new invention does not necessarily imply either acceptance or widespread use. In ancient Mexico, for instance, the concept of the wheel was known – wheeled toys have been found in Veracruz – but wheels were not used for vehicles. The lack of large beasts of burden was probably a major reason, as we saw in Chapter One. Western Europe provides a more recent example: many of Leonardo da Vinci's inventions, such as his sketches of an airplane, were not experimented with because society at that time was simply not ready for such an innovation. In other words, questions of the origins of new ideas in material or non-material culture are subordinate to the larger questions of why they are accepted (or why not), and what the short and long-term consequences of such an acceptance were.

The current consensus among archaeologists concerned with the development of ancient Mexican civilization is that no significant transoceanic influences can be identified prior to the coming of the Spanish. Nor is there evidence for the ancient Mexicans influencing other civilizations across the seas. The growth of Mexican civilization was essentially independent, although ancient Mexico was certainly in contact with other peoples in the Americas, both to the south, in Central America, and to the north, in northern Mexico and the American Southwest. The idea of working metals such as copper, for instance, appears to have originated in South America and was brought by coastal traders to the west coast of Mexico from either Peru/Ecuador or Panama; there is a long history of development in the latter areas and none in ancient Mexico. From West Mexico metallurgy spread to the Toltec empire in the tenth century AD. The Maya of the Northern Lowlands also traded with lower Central America for gold and copper from Terminal Classic times (AD 800–1000) onwards. In addition, there is good evidence of trade between Mexico and the Southwest, with items such as turquoise moving south, and macaws to the north. We have seen, too, that groups like the Toltecs traded with Central America for polychrome ceramics.

Much debate, however, still focuses on the extent, importance, and dating of these trading contacts that aided not only the movements of goods, such as obsidian which was traded all over Mesoamerica, but also of ideas, such as the popularity of deities like Tlaloc the rain god. The general trajectory of complex developments in Mexico points to cultural precedents of all the major changes in this trajectory, and furthermore it is comparable with growth trends in other parts of the pre-industrial world. Although it is possible, if not probable, therefore, that there were occasional landings of foreign peoples on the shores of ancient Mexico, or overland contacts with foreign groups, such landings or contacts apparently had little effect on the general development of Mexican civilization.

In a more general vein, archaeologists now know, on the basis of a huge quantity of recent field research around the globe, that complex societies developed not in one or two places but independently in at least half a dozen throughout human history. The question is thus not who influenced whom, but what cultural processes led to the development of complexity in all these places, from the rise of large cities and the state in fourth millennium BC Mesopotamia to the emergence of the state in lowland valleys of Peru around the time of Christ. As we have seen, archaeologists today are more interested in *why* changes took place, why some innovations were accepted and others not, rather than in whether the innovations were local or introduced from the outside; they want to know if it is possible to detect general principles at work (general "laws") in the evolutionary development of human culture.

What led people in different places in the Old and New Worlds to become increasingly sedentary in their ways of life, practicing agriculture and animal domestication and slowly giving up the nomadic hunting and gathering that had characterized the overwhelming bulk of human history? What were the factors involved in the rise of chiefs and the increasing inequality in human cultures through time? Why do the trajectories of the growth of pre-industrial complex societies through time and space look remarkably similar, even though these cultural developments took place in quite different environments? Why, for example, in Mesopotamia, the Indus Valley, and the Andes of South America, as well as at Monte Alban as we have seen above, do cities appear to result from very rapid population growth, as recently argued by the archaeologist Henry Wright, rather than from a slow build up of population? To try to understand such cultural processes archaeologists need to consider not only what caused these similar patterns, but also what may have led to the specific differences in each case. Studying these questions may eventually show whether there were general laws at work in human antiquity.

Each question has produced varying answers in the scholarly literature. In recent years, however, most analyses of cultural complexity have adopted the systems thinking that is so much a part of our world today. That is, archaeologists have turned away from quests to find single, overriding causal factors in the rise of complex societies in general, and cities in particular, and have instead tried to explain this phenomenon by looking at the interactions of a series of factors in specific cultural and ecological contexts.

Factors thought to influence cultural complexity are environment, population increase, trade and markets, warfare, and technological innovation. Some variables – such as population increase – always seem to be present, but they are not, on their own, sufficient to explain the development of complex societies. One of the most stimulating of the recent systemic examinations of the growth of complexity has been made by the archaeologist Kent Flannery. In an article entitled "The Cultural Evolution of Civilizations," Flannery focused on the role of information processing by segments (subsystems) of societies, and how changes in the access to and handling and control of information can lead to the evolution of socio-political complexity. Flannery emphasized two processes that can lead to the evolution of complexity: increasing *segregation* ("the amount of internal differentiation and specialization of subsystems");[16] and growing *centralization* ("the degree of linkage between the various subsystems and the highest order controls in society").[17] In addition, he identified two mechanisms that help bring about change. The first is *promotion* which occurs when an institution increases in importance over time; an example would be the promotion of the role of a temporary war chief who emerges only at times of conflict into the role of a permanent military leader with greatly increased powers. The second mechanism Flannery identified is *linearization*, where the bypassing of lower order controls leads to centralization. For instance, central authority ("the state") may take over the control of irrigation from local leaders during times of warfare, and then when peace returns, the central authority retains the power.

Flannery offered a series of examples of how various socio-environmental stresses, such as warfare or population pressure, can in different cases lead to promotion and/or linearization. He also provided a model for such changes and indicated how it might be used in the future to simulate the rise of complexity. Finally, in recent publications, Flannery and Joyce Marcus have also emphasized the crucial role that changes in ideology play (e.g. a change from "we are equal" to "some are tied to the supernatural and therefore have the right to special privileges"). Unfortunately, surprisingly few scholars have followed up these leads and attempted to indicate what more detailed working "rules" that govern the development of complexity might look like.

In an important review of the subject,[18] Henry Wright argues that in examining different sequences of state development in preindustrial societies, including ancient Mexico, one important pattern that consistently emerges is competition and conflict among elites. Such competition had ramifications in a variety of economic, political, and ideological arenas that systemically reinforced each other. For example, the procurement of desired raw materials, such as obsidian, and their eventual distribution both locally and distantly through trade, clearly involved control of these resources and in turn necessitated the control of labor and its organization in order to mine, carry, work, and distribute the raw material. The coercion of neighboring groups might be a necessary part of this process. Wright further argues that the emergence of state societies is relatively rapid and is marked by the development of three or four levels of hierarchical authority (what Wright terms "control").

In a brief, preliminary examination of the survey data from the Valley of Oaxaca, Wright argues that the available information does fit the general patterning he has found in his reviews of the data from Mesopotamia, the Indus Valley, and the Andes. The two growth spurts at Monte Alban, just after 500 BC and just before the time of Christ, come at periods when there is strong inferential evidence in the archaeological record for conflict, and they coincide with the development of first three and then four levels of control hierarchy. Rapid nucleation of population occurs with the first spurt and the construction of palatial residences with the second.

Wright contends that scholars must now focus on the detailed analyses of the specific conditions under which competition operated so as to identify, where possible, recurring patterns. If this is successful, they could then examine which conditions lead to population nucleation and the rapid growth of complexity, and which do not. Certainly this approach would be worth investigating further.

To summarize, there have been many attempts in the current archaeological literature to answer the question of what led to the rise of cities and the growth of complex societies. Some are sweeping, such as that population pressure led people to change their lifeways, while others are specific, arguing that a particular natural phenomenon – like a volcanic eruption – may have triggered major changes. Many archaeologists are now trying to identify cultural processes that affected past civilizations and are attempting to produce testable statements about how cultures change given certain environmental parameters. As the archaeological data base increases, field and analytic techniques improve, and methodologies become more exacting and sophisticated, so our understanding of the causes of urbanism will advance.

The origins of new cultural traits, however, are just a small part of these general concerns and not the overriding focus of the discipline as some popular books might lead one to believe. Moreover, given the current interest in the evolutionary development of human culture, questions about why changes occur and the nature of their impact supersede those about where such changes originate, so that archaeologists working in Mexico want to know why the wheel never had any importance in Precolumbian times rather than whether it was locally invented or introduced from afar.

Let us now turn from "why" concerns to critical questions of "how" archaeologists interpret their data.

PART III

How do we know?

CHAPTER TEN

Reconstructing the Past

How can archaeologists look at piles of stones and say that they are houses or, more particularly, houses where peasants lived? How do they know that weaving was important at a certain site, or the number of people who lived there? The archaeological record cannot speak to us like a modern anthropologist's informant. It is mute. Moreover, it is a very incomplete record that has usually been disturbed over long periods of time. How can archaeologists begin to understand this static record that remains today? How can they link cultural actions in ancient times with these modern remains? Although these kinds of questions are clearly very basic, archaeologists still cannot agree on how to answer them. I will try to explore some of these questions in the context of the development of the ancient cities of Mexico.

When someone asks an archaeologist, "How do you know that?" the unspoken question they are asking is, how do archaeologists make the intellectual leap from, say, lines of rocks and broken pieces of pottery to discussions of houses where different classes of people with varying occupations lived? In other words, how do scholars "interpret" the archaeological record they uncover on and beneath the ground?

One approach an archaeologist uses is to undertake an intuitive analysis, drawing on the resemblances among archaeological materials in the published literature, sites he or she has personally examined, and the data that are currently being analyzed. All these "interpretations" are based on implicit or explicit analogies.

Analogies are the critical aspect of archaeological attempts to "flesh out" the static record that has survived to this day. *The American Heritage Dictionary* defines "analogy" as an "inference that if two things are alike in some respects they must be alike in others," with "infer" meaning "to draw a conclusion." In archaeological interpretation, analogies are used that range from the most simple correlations to exceedingly complex formulations.

A simple analogy may be used by an archaeologist when, for example, he or she interprets a single row of stones in the shape of a rectangle, with a stone-lined burned area inside the rectangle, as the remains of a house made originally of wood. The archaeologist is using the similarity in a few aspects between the archaeological remains and modern houses made of perishable materials as a warrant to project the other aspects of the modern houses onto the archaeological record. Finding additional correspondences, such as a deposit with broken pottery and animal bones behind the stone rectangle, which would be interpreted through analogy as a domestic refuse dump, would further strengthen confidence in the overall analogy.

A variant of this kind of analogy would be the interpretation of a multi-roomed stone walled and roofed range structure in the Maya Lowlands as a palace where elite personages resided. In this case, a general analogy has been made to other historically known civilizations, such as ancient Greece, where the elite rulers lived in elaborate multi-roomed palaces situated near their great temples. While this

111 Inside the Palace at Palenque. With images of Classical Greek or Roman palaces in their minds, some archaeologists found it hard to believe that the Maya elite could have lived in the dank and dark multi-roomed structures called "palaces" in the Maya Lowlands.

particular interpretation was generally accepted and became part of traditional discussions of ancient Maya society, some scholars challenged it. They looked at the relatively dark and dank rooms, for example, and contended that nobody would have wanted to live in them. They used their own modern sensibilities to warrant their argument. To this group, the palaces were public buildings that were used for a variety of activities such as changing rooms for priests and rulers where they could don ceremonial garb prior to major festivals.

Who was right? Until recently, when assessing the validity of an analogy the experience and background of the archaeologist carried more weight than the nature of the inference itself. This was particularly the case if the inference was subjective, such as, no powerful ruler would want to live in rooms that are perceived today as inhospitable and unfitting. This statement was made by the late Sir J. Eric Thompson, justly regarded as the "doyen" of Mayanists and one of the most knowledgeable scholars of his day, so that clearly his opinion was highly valued. There is, however, no one answer to this particular problem since, on the basis of architectual features, artifactual associations, and spatial contexts, it appears that "palace" is not just one kind of building. It is a useless term because it includes a variety of different structures with numerous functions. Moreover, as archaeologist Peter Harrison's research at Tikal showed, many "palaces" were probably multi-functional as well as multi-roomed.

There is an inherent danger with the use of analogy in that, over time, the speculativeness of the approach may be lost so that the analogy becomes an accepted fact. Instead of the original "x might be interpreted as y on the basis of a particular analogy," archaeologists begin to say "x is y." The original analogy is forgotten. In some instances the equation $x = y$ may seem quite reasonable. A series of connected furrows next to a site clearly were irrigation canals, or two parallel rectangular buildings must have been a ball court. Such interpretations helped advance the situation whereby interpretation became fact, and as this change in usage spread from "safe" inferences to more problematical ones potential variability was often overlooked. For example, because archaeologists did not "see" many houses around the remains of the huge buildings at Classic Maya sites, these places were viewed as non-urban ceremonial centers. It was not until the basic mapping data was published by the University of Pennsylvania archaeologists at the site of Tikal, which clearly revealed the remains of numerous perishable domestic structures in the 16 square kilometers around the central core, that this traditional interpretation was demolished.

Unfortunately, as field methods and laboratory analyses improved, as more information about ancient remains was collected, and as new interpretive models became significantly more complex and sophisticated, interpretation frequently became more intuitive and stipulative. While it might be possible to call a flat-topped pyramid crowned by a single-roomed building a religious temple, the analogical waters became much murkier when a large cleared area was labeled a "marketplace," or a long building a "men's house," yet such inferences were continually being made. What, in fact, would a trading center, or manufacturing areas, let alone a growing bureaucracy or a standing army, really look like in the archaeological record? As data about the

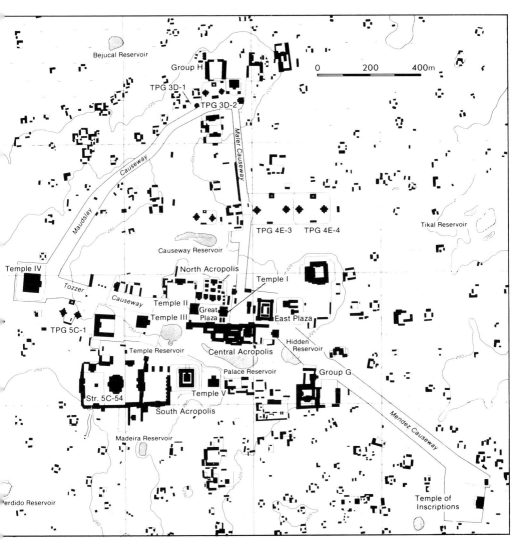

112 Map of the center of the Maya city of Tikal. The true urban
character of ancient Maya sites like Tikal only became clear when new
surveys and excavations revealed dense concentrations of domestic
buildings around the ceremonial core.

past became more complex so did the "messages" that the "facts" of
the archaeological record "spoke" to the archaeologists. It is no wonder
that different scholars began to present opposing interpretations of
identical archaeological material.

A strong bias also began to develop towards what were termed
"direct historical analogies," where comparisons were made between
the archaeological record and cultures that were perceived to be

historical descendants of the ancient culture. These analogies were deemed to be more reliable than more "general" analogies. While the direct historical analogies might well be very persuasive, particularly when arguments were made for broad cultural stability through time, this approach presented several problems. First, continuity does not necessarily mean stability, so that an assumption that because a case could be made for a cultural link between past and present then analogies between them were "safe" was not necessarily a good one. Second, the analogical reasoning was sometimes quite circular. The "facts" of the archaeological record, often intuitive analogies, might reveal a pattern. This pattern would then be compared with the ethnographic record, and the accuracy of this comparison would be tested against the original archaeological "facts." The circularity of this procedure was missed many times because the original interpretive analogies (the "facts") were not recognized explicitly by archaeologists. Third, the potential power of general analogies was not usually appreciated and this source of linking theory was significantly underutilized for many years, owing to the anti-comparative, anti-evolutionary bias that dominated American archaeology in this century up to recent times.

By the 1970s, archaeology was in a real dilemma. More and more data were being recovered yet interpretations and "explanations" of the past, and the meaning of the record, were the subject of an increasing controversy that appeared to be leading not to new insights but to non-productive dead-ends.

In recent years, this trend fortunately seems to have been stalled because archaeologists have begun to realize that they must pay closer attention to methodology. It is not those who hear the messages of the archaeological record who must be evaluated but rather the very nature of the messages and the "facts" that are seen to "speak" to them. How can systematic approaches to the data be made so that they are open to consistent evaluation? The most persuasive answer is, in simplest terms, to improve and make rigorous the analogies that are used to link the static archaeological record of today with dynamic activities of the past. This approach has been labeled "middle-range," "bridging," or "linking" theory in archaeological writings.

The first step towards improving our archaeological methodology is to increase the quality of relevant data upon which persuasive analogies can be made. The principal problem in the past has been that ethnographers have often not provided the kind of information, particularly about material culture, that is of use to archaeologists. To deal with this problem, archaeologists have had to undertake ethno-graphic field research themselves. Such studies – ethnoarchaeology – allow archaeologists to focus specifically on the kinds of cultural activities of immediate concern to them, and to look at both the material consequences of these activities and their wider environmental contexts.

Graduate students with whom I have worked are increasingly using ethnoarchaeological data in their research, focusing on such questions as storage activities in complex societies; the use of garden space around peasant houses; and the nature of craft specialization. These students have worked with modern Maya farmers in Northern Yucatan, and farmers and craftspeople in the Tuxtla Mountains region in the Gulf Coast Lowlands. Their studies clearly improved their ability to link patterns found in the archaeological record with past activities.

Another variable that has to be taken into account when creating a rigorous methodology is that many processes may have influenced the formation of the archaeological record from the time that material items were deposited in the ground until the present day. Geological processes such as erosion or earthquakes; activities of animals like earthworms or moles; and human behavior, such as the reuse of tools, are just three examples. Long-term, intermittent reuse of sites will leave different archaeological records than sites that have only been used for a short period of time. Archaeologists must be trained to identify and understand the various factors that influence the makeup of the record we view today.

A further approach to increased analogical rigor is the detailed use of historical records. When rich historical documentation about cultural activities exists, ethnohistoric research has helped archaeologists link historically observed activities with the material patterns left in the ground. For example, as part of our archaeological studies on the island of Cozumel, off the east coast of the Yucatan peninsula, David Freidel and I were able to utilize historical descriptions of buildings and their uses, written by the Spanish at the time of the sixteenth-century Conquest, to aid our understanding of the remains of Precolumbian structures that dated to a couple of centuries earlier. We were able to relate the use of space and structural form in certain contexts described in the Spanish documents to comparable forms found archaeologically on Cozumel in similar contexts. The chroniclers of the early Spanish explorers such as Córdoba, Grijalva, and Cortés, who all visited Yucatan, might have described, for example, an elite residence as having open, colonnaded front rooms, and back rooms with restricted access; the description might go on to note that the front rooms had a more public function while the back ones were private. Thus, we were able to make inferential arguments about the different functions of a wide variety of buildings that we were studying that might, under less favorable circumstances, have all been generically labeled "palaces" or "shrines."

Although Cozumel is an example of "direct" analogy, historical documents can be used in a more general manner, as well. In the Maya area, for example, some scholars have looked at widescale settlement patterning and have linked it with a "feudal" pattern described in the historical records of medieval Europe. Unfortunately, the finding of two similar patterns, no matter how close or far away they are in time and space, explains nothing. *If* a theoretical argument can be mounted that explains patterning in the (relatively) known case (that is, historical feudalism in Europe), *and* a rigorous analogical argument can be built up linking the known example with the ancient one, *then* it may be possible to explain the causes of the ancient patterning.

Such a "general" strategy has important implications for archaeological research designs. Instead of the traditional sequence of (1) going to the field to collect "facts"; (2) putting the facts in chronological order and "fleshing out" the sequence so as to create a culture historical picture based on the facts; and (3) trying to explain the whys and wherefores of the sequence by building a theory, it is clear that archaeologists would probably be better off if they (1) discovered patterns in data already collected or which they collect; (2) build linking theory through ethnoarchaeological and/or ethnohistorical research; and then (3) after meaning has been given to the archaeological record, attempt to test more general theories of culture change and to build culture history. In other words, fieldwork and the writing of culture history might well come towards the later rather than the earlier stages of a long-term research program. Obviously, however, there must be constant interplay between the more immediate goals of research at each stage, and the need to build long-term theory. "How do we know?" becomes a critical *explicit* step in the research procedure and not a hidden, subjective one.

CHAPTER ELEVEN

Reconstructing Ancient Mexico

Mexico has proved a rich source for analogies because of the wide variety of historic and ethnographic materials available in the literature and the many opportunities for ethnoarchaeological research that it presents in its varying environments.

The possibilities of direct historical linkages are particularly strong for the Aztecs in Central Mexico; the Maya in Southern Mesoamerica; and the Zapotecs and Mixtecs in Oaxaca. Accounts by the Spanish conquistadors and the early civilians, especially the clerics, who followed them in the early to mid-sixteenth century provide many details about the Native American civilizations at the time of European contacts. While scholars must be ever aware of the biases of the Spanish writers, and of the changes induced by the Conquest that would already have occurred when some writers observed the Native American peoples, the accounts still provide many details of the native populations which can be linked with material remains in the archaeological record of the early sixteenth century. For example, Bishop Landa's published study of Yucatan, and Fray Bernardino de Sahagún's multi-volume *General History of the Things of New Spain*, are major sixteenth-century sources for direct analogies about the Maya and the Aztec, respectively.

Greater problems in archaeological research in Mexico occur, however, when historical data from Conquest times are linked to the pre-Conquest archaeological record on the grounds of direct historical connections. The problems have principally arisen when Aztec cultural activities or institutions have been projected into the past without secure analogical links. The Aztec merchants who participated in long-distance trade, for example, were organized into groups known as *pochteca*. But that does not mean that the presence of long-distance trade among the Olmec, Teotihuacanos, or Toltecs automatically indicates that these peoples had *pochteca*. A clear, analogical argu-

113 (*left*) **Spanish sources** Sixteenth-century Spanish writers, such as Fray Bernardino de Sahagún, have provided much useful information about the Aztecs and Maya at the time of the Conquest. These drawings from Sahagún show Aztec featherworking. See ill. 96.

114 (*above*) **Evidence from ethnography** Studies of modern Mesoamericans, such as these Maya villagers in front of their thatched-roof home, provide useful analogical data about the past.

ment would have to be mounted, not just an assertion of historical continuity from, say, the Toltecs to the Aztecs.

Such problems are compounded when modern ethnographic data are used to "interpret" ancient remains in Mexico. Direct historical analogies from modern to Precolumbian times are difficult to argue given both the significant cultural disruptions caused by the Spanish Conquest and the huge changes wrought by new technologies and the current world economy. This does not mean that the rich ethnographic literature available for modern Mexico, or the multitude of possibilities for current ethnographic research in, for example, the Maya area, Oaxaca, or Central Mexico, should be ignored. Rather, instead of justifying analogies that link the archaeological record with modern data through their putative historical associations, it might make more sense to support the analogies by arguing that similar ecological situations will produce equivalent adaptations. Such general analogies are not necessarily "weaker" than direct historical analogies, and, in many cases, may be easier to support. For instance, studies of agricultural practices among modern peasants in tropical environments may hold the best keys for interpreting the use of space around the often-enigmatic "house mounds" of the Classic Maya in the Southern Lowlands.

Having considered how both direct historical analogies and more general analogies may be applied to ancient Mexico, what tangible remains have the Precolumbian peoples left behind which may help us interpret the archaeological record? Because some of the peoples were literate, a small number of written native documents, such as the four Maya codices (fold-out, screen-like books), have survived the ravages of time and the Spanish Conquest. These primary materials have been used to interpret and amplify the archaeological record, but, unfortunately, they are too few and fragmentary to be of more than limited use. The Maya codices, for example, are principally concerned with what we might label today as astrological portents. Nevertheless, they do contain other information, such as the depiction of ceramic vessels and incense burners in the Dresden Codex.

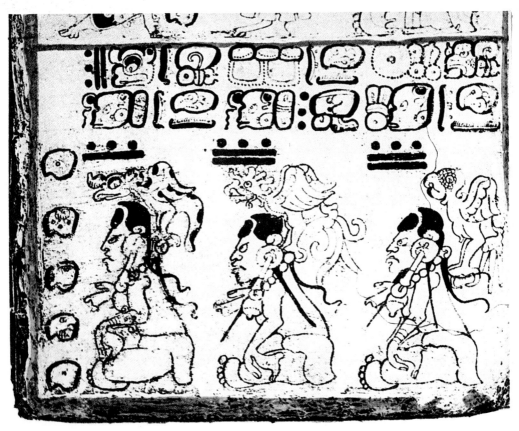

115 (*left*) **Native documents** Four Maya codices are among the few native written records to have survived. But they are of only limited help to the archaeologist: this page from the Dresden Codex discusses how to cure seizures caused by the moon.

116,117 **Evidence of the explorers** Drawings left us by nineteenth-century artists, such as Frederick Catherwood (arch at Labna, *above*), lend life to ancient Mexican ruins. They also provide a source of evidence to set alongside more recent photographs (*above right*; see also ill. 65).

118 (*right*) **Maya decipherment** Lintel 24 at Yaxchilan is a prime example of a scene that can now be "read" thanks to the recent decipherment of Maya glyphs. Epigrapher Linda Schele and art historian Mary Ellen Miller argue that the lintel represents a bloodletting rite that took place on 28 October 709. The king, Shield Jaguar, stands with a blazing torch before the kneeling figure of his wife, Lady Xoc, who pulls a thorn-lined rope through her tongue.

Inscriptions on stone and pottery, however, have been increasingly helpful in providing information about ancient Mexican peoples. For example, key breakthroughs by glyphic experts in the decipherment of Maya writing, such as the readings of historic texts that talk about the military exploits of particular rulers, have had significant impacts on archaeological understandings of Classic Maya civilization, particularly those that relate to the Maya elite and their activities.

The rich remains of sculpture, figurines, murals, and graffiti have also provided information that can be used to interpret patterns in the archaeological data. Both architectural and freestanding sculpture depict images showing details – such as clothing and weapons – that can be used in interpreting archaeological remains. Architectural carvings, such as the illustration of a thatched hut on the façade of the Great Arch at the Puuc site of Labna, help give insight into remains that have long since perished.

119 (*left*) **Murals** Surviving wall paintings provide important information not only about particular historical events but also about houses, weapons and the practice of warfare. This detail of a mural from the Temple of the Warriors, Chichen Itza, depicts warriors attacking a village or town.

120 (*right*). **Figurines** Ceramic portraits of ancient Mexicans yield useful evidence for clothing and tools. Those from the island of Jaina – like the one shown here – are famous for their fine craftsmanship. Unfortunately most were looted and their archaeological contexts are unknown.

Figurines showing individuals undertaking varying tasks can also provide a framework for analogy. The figurines from the island of Jaina, for example, show activities such as the grinding of corn. Tools shown on the figurines can be used in analogical interpretations of the functions of comparable objects in the archaeological record.

Well-preserved murals are another important source of information, as are graffiti. The paintings at Teotihuacan, Cacaxtla, Bonampak, and Chichen Itza, as well as the graffiti scratched on the temple walls at Tikal, have all offered details that can be used to help interpret the archaeological record; the murals at Chichen Itza, for example, show us how certain weapons were used at that site and, by extension, perhaps at other Maya sites. Such depictions can then be used in analogical interpretations of stone artifacts.

To summarize, ethnographic data, Conquest Period documents, and artistic and historical evidence from Precolumbian times can all be used in the interpretation of archaeological remains. The potential of these sources is huge as long as archaeologists are aware of the pitfalls when using such approaches. In certain cases, the most secure basis for analogical arguments may not be direct historical links, however, but instead more general analogies comparing similarities in adaptive settings. The interpretive potential of information from other complex societies throughout the world, therefore, in both past and current times, from feudal Europe to recent states in Africa, must also be taken into account.

CHAPTER TWELVE

Reconstructing Life in the Cities

Let us now turn a critical eye to the vignettes of ancient Mexican life that were presented in Chapters Two through Eight. How was I able to reconstruct the activities I described in these brief sketches? What were the bases for some of the analogies I used in my interpretations and what inferences were more speculative? Clearly, given the current state of the art, many of the analogies are of the impressionistic kind that I have just analyzed above and that I argued need to be strengthened if the field is to advance. So, where possible, in the discussions below, I will try to indicate what specific directions scholars might take to improve such analogies. I am more interested in discussing the ways in which archaeologists make inferences rather than in how accurate or "good" the reconstructions are.

San Lorenzo

The reconstruction of a day in the life of a weaver living near San Lorenzo is based principally on the research at that site conducted by Michael Coe and his colleagues, and reported in Coe's and Richard Diehl's two-volume monograph, *In the Land of the Olmec*. Coe and Diehl undertook both archaeological and ethnographic research at San Lorenzo. Although the modern inhabitants of the region have no historical connections with the ancient Olmecs, general analogies between the two can be justified by their nearly identical ecological situations. Coe and Diehl contend that climate and environmental conditions of the past at San Lorenzo were essentially the same as those of today. They further argue that the preferences for soil use and perhaps for agricultural practices were also quite similar.

Obviously, much of this reconstruction, and of the others too, is at best informed speculation. But many aspects of it are based on analogies to the available archaeological data.

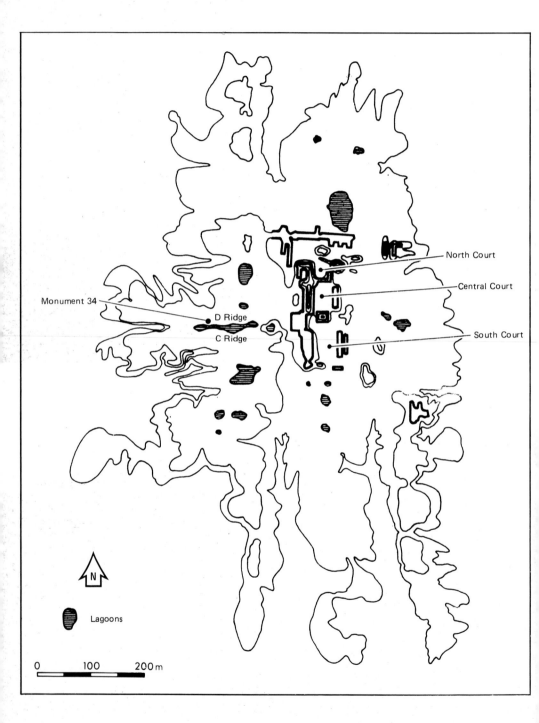

North Court

Central Court

Monument 34

South Court

D Ridge

C Ridge

N

Lagoons

0   100   200 m

San Lorenzo and ethnoarchaeology

121–123 Ethnographic research has provided useful analogical evidence to help us understand past exploitation of the environment. For example, houses at the village of Potrero Nuevo, near San Lorenzo (*right*), give us some insight into the likely building materials used by the Olmecs. Similarly houselot excavation, as conducted in an ethnoarchaeological research program by Thomas Killion in the Tuxtlas region of the Gulf Coast (*below*), may help show how villagers used the space available to them. All this can add further detail to the more conventional archaeological plan of San Lorenzo achieved by surface survey and excavation (*left*), which shows the construction of the site on top of an artificially leveled ridge.

On the banks of the river, to the north of San Lorenzo, Coe and Diehl found extensive remains that they called a large village; the village, however, was not excavated. Other excavations produced artifacts whose forms suggest spindle whorls, from which it can be inferred that the ancient inhabitants of San Lorenzo undertook weaving. Some of the diet of these people can also be inferred from remains found in the excavations, including animal bones, and by analogy with the food-stuffs available in the region today.

Trace-element analysis of the basalt monuments located at the ceremonial center of San Lorenzo on top of an artificially leveled hill indicates that the stone was obtained in the Tuxtla Mountains some distance away. Some of the monuments found weighed more than 20 tons. It is assumed that they were moved on wooden rollers to nearby waterways, and then floated on rafts. There is no direct evidence to support this assumption, but it seems the most efficient and logical of all the alternatives. At San Lorenzo, Coe and Diehl discovered evidence for an earthen ramp that could have been used to haul the monuments from the river to the top of the hill. Given the relatively small population of San Lorenzo, based on the limited number of domestic remains found near the center, it can be inferred that the city's rulers must have drawn on the inhabitants of a number of neighboring villages to provide the workforce for the large labor-intensive projects associated with the main site.

Clearly, one approach that would increase our understanding of Olmec village life would be the careful horizontal excavation of a series of peasant houses in the San Lorenzo region. But, just as importantly, a follow-up study to Coe and Diehl's ethnographic/ecological research is needed; in particular, an ethnoarchaeological examination of peasant households would be helpful. In the nearby Tuxtla Mountains, archaeologist Thomas Killion completed a pioneering ethnoarchaeol-ogical study that examined the size and organization of space in and around households in relation to the size and location of infield and outfield agricultural plots. Through excavation he also studied the diversity and quantity of the material remains in the various parts of the houselots outside the houses themselves. He found clear pat-terning of these remains in relation to the presence or absence of infield plots (located close to the houselots) and the distance of outfield ones cultivated by the household. In simplified terms, one finding was that households with infield plots had more constricted houselot space and kept these spaces relatively clear by pushing or sweeping garbage and debris to the sides of the lots. Such ethnoarchaeological work holds much promise for providing more useful data for analogies that will help elucidate ancient patterns. For example, if the archaeologist were to excavate what could be identified as an ancient houselot and found a certain kind of pattern in the material remains uncovered (perhaps a cleared zone with a particular sort of discarded material towards the fringes), then he or she might be in a position to argue by analogy that that household had emphasized infield agriculture and did not cultivate more distant outfield plots.

Monte Alban

The principal function for Structure J is suggested by the carved panels found along its base. These contain inscriptions citing different towns or regions conquered by Monte Alban. The archaeologist Joyce Marcus has identified nearly a dozen of the towns mentioned on these panels. The building thus appears to have been a monument to Monte Alban's military successes and was built by its rulers to commemorate their victories.

The building may have had other functions as well. For example, it appears to have had an astronomical alignment. The inferential argument for the astronomical significance of Structure J is not based on typical ethnographic or historic analogies but is nonetheless convincing. First, the building's arrowhead-like shape is very rare. Only one other similar example, from a nearby site in Oaxaca, has been found in ancient Mexico. Second, the building is oriented differently from all the other structures around it. Clearly some factor was strong enough to override the regular orientation that might have been expected. The archaeoastronomer Anthony Aveni has argued that the structure's peculiar orientation may relate to the fact that the front doorway of Structure J is perpendicularly aligned to a point on the horizon where the bright star Capella would have had its first rising in the dawn sky (technically called its heliacal rising) on the same day that the sun would have reached its first zenith point over Monte Alban (at the time that Structure J was built: in a period just before the time of Christ). Third, the front stairway of Structure J is perpendicularly aligned with Structure P, and more particularly with the exit hole of a unique vertical shaft in Structure P that emanates from the interior chamber in the latter building. At the zenith of the sun, it would shine

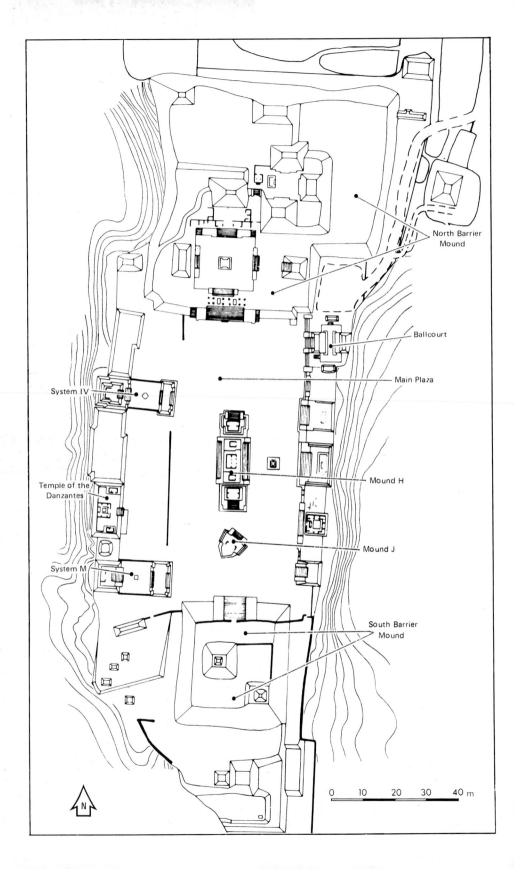

North Barrier
Mound

Ballcourt

Main Plaza

System IV

Mound H

Temple of the
Danzantes

Mound J

System M

South Barrier
Mound

N

0   10   20   30   40 m

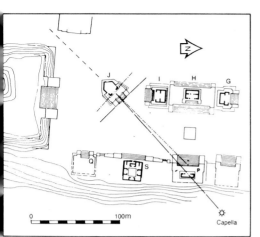

Archaeoastronomy at Monte Alban

124–127 The special orientation and arrow-like shape of Structure J at Monte Alban (*left* and *below*) led archaeoastronomer Anthony Aveni to hypothesize that the building was deliberately oriented towards the bright star Capella at its rising point on the horizon (*above left*). The main function for Structure J as a monument to success in battle is suggested by the carved panels found along its base (*above right*): these show names of different towns or regions conquered by Monte Alban.

directly down the shaft with no shadow in the inner chamber. It is difficult to imagine that the alignments were purely coincidental, especially given their connectedness. Fourth, several other alignments have been suggested for the structure. Additional supporting evidence is provided by crossed-stick symbols found on Structure J that may represent astronomical sighting sticks.

The inference about the commemorative function of Structure J would be strengthened if new excavations revealed sacrificial burial in or around the building. Mesoamerican peoples frequently marked their success on the battlefield with sacrificial events. Additional decipherments of Zapotec writing might also illuminate this argument.

It would be hard to strengthen the astronomical inferences for Structure J except by the finding of additional alignments, and perhaps by the discovery of artifacts whose function could be analogically identified as being of astronomical use. While archaeoastronomical research used to be looked on askance by many archaeologists, the careful studies undertaken in recent years by a growing body of scholars has made the ascription of astronomical functions to various buildings much more plausible.

Teotihuacan

A series of research projects by North American and Mexican scholars in both Teotihuacan and the surrounding region have greatly increased our knowledge of that ancient city in the past three decades. The huge survey program directed by the archaeologist René Millon has resulted in a comprehensive map of the whole city showing both its vast extent (an area of over 20 square kilometers at its apogee), and its great complexity.

A particularly interesting discovery at Teotihuacan is a residential compound that Millon has identified as a Oaxacan *barrio*. The discovery here not only of Oaxacan pottery, but also of Oaxacan architecture and iconography has led scholars to infer that the compound housed a group of Oaxacans and functioned in some manner as an embassy or foreign enclave. Another compound has tentatively been identified as a merchants' *barrio* principally on the basis of many non-local ceramics, but clearly this identification must remain speculative without further research, particularly excavations directed towards the uncovering of data that could be related to "foreign" inhabitants. Analogies drawn from studies of foreign

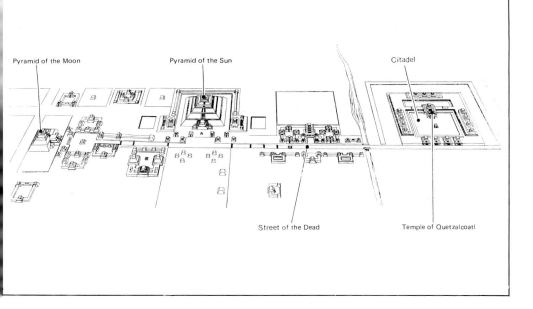

Pyramid of the Moon

Pyramid of the Sun

Citadel

Street of the Dead

Temple of Quetzalcoatl

128,129 **Teotihuacan** View and plan of the central core of the city. The plan shows the many smaller structures around the major monuments revealed by the huge survey program undertaken by René Millon and his colleagues.

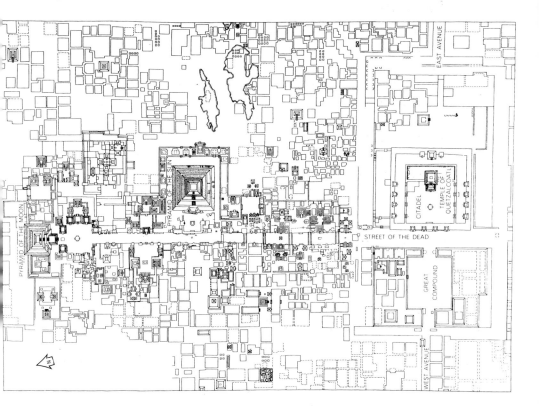

PYRAMID OF THE MOON

PYRAMID OF THE SUN

EAST AVENUE

CITADEL

TEMPLE OF QUETZALCOATL

STREET OF THE DEAD

GREAT COMPOUND

WEST AVENUE

N

enclaves in historically documented cities might help archaeologists to plan such research strategies.

Millon's investigations clearly indicate that Teotihuacan was a manufacturing center for a variety of products, particularly obsidian. A source of a distinctive, high-quality green obsidian lies nearby, as do sources of more typical gray obsidian. A number of obsidian workshop areas have been identified at the ancient city by the Millon team, particularly by the archaeologist Michael Spence. It has, however, been questioned as to whether all these sites represent craft production, and Spence recently has been more conservative in his firm identifications. The problem appears to be that there are no clear criteria on which all archaeologists can agree for recognizing an obsidian production locale. To put this problem in a broader context, the question is plainly, how can archaeologists unambiguously identify craft specialization in the archaeological record and get away from impressionistic designations? This is an area where ethnoarchaeology plays a vital role.

Archaeologist Philip Arnold undertook an ethnoarchaeological study of pottery manufacture in the Tuxtla Mountains of the Gulf Coast of Mexico as part of the Matacapan project, a study of a large urban center that apparently had close ties with Teotihuacan. Arnold examined the material reflections of ceramic workshops and was able

130 **Pottery-making** Debris from modern ceramic manufacturing in the Tuxtlas region of the Gulf Coast of Mexico – which probably had close ties with Teotihuacan – has been used by Philip Arnold to provide clues to the location of manufacturing zones in Precolumbian times.

to find a series of related traits, including tools and debris from failed firings, that can be used as signatures for the presence of manufacturing zones. Moreover, he was able to relate the workshops to the use of space in households and to more general economic processes. To give just one small example of what his research has shown, while it has often been assumed that the use of kilns to fire pottery is a direct reflection of growing intensity of production, Arnold found that availability of space surrounding a house may also play a critical role in the decision as to whether or not to use a kiln. Further research of this kind should allow archaeologists to take the signatures back to the archaeological record and settle some of the controversies over identifiable production sites.

The exact role of merchants in Teotihuacan and the nature of trade both in and out of the city is still an open question, but we do know that there was contact with all parts of ancient Mexico, including Monte Alban. Recent studies of the energetics and economics of long-distance transportation of manufactured materials from Teotihuacan are offering plausible and testable models that can serve as guidelines for future research on the city's role as an economic center. The archaeologist Robert Drennan, for example, in examining possible reasons for the Late Preclassic development of complexity, has argued that, given the distances between major centers, the long-distance trade of foodstuffs would not have become profitable until Early Classic times when the population reached sufficiently high density levels to create large potential markets, and that trade would not have had a significant impact on the growth of complexity until this period.

Cerros

This vignette is based on recent field research by archaeologists David Freidel and Robin Robertson from Southern Methodist University. Their work, particularly Robertson's careful ceramic analysis, has shown that virtually all the major construction and occupation at Cerros dates to the Late Preclassic Period. Stratigraphic excavations indicate that, prior to 50 BC, Cerros was a modest village with a small ceremonial center. Between 50 BC and AD 100, the site underwent rapid change that included what the excavators have termed "urban renewal," with a large part of the former village razed to make way for a large architectural complex. The pyramids that form a portion of this complex were built at the same time, although there were subsequent

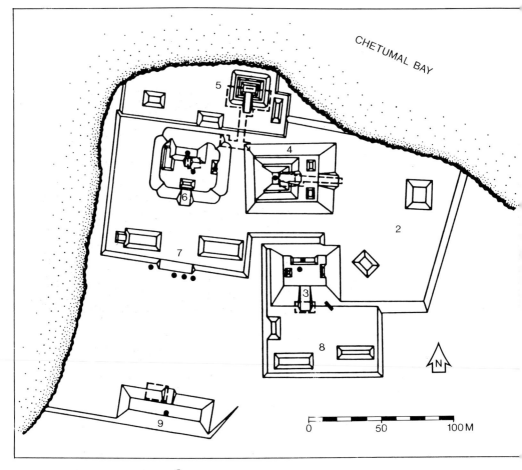

CHETUMAL BAY

131–133 **Cerros and coastal trade** The plan (*left*) shows the main structures (2–9) in the ceremonial center of the town. An air photograph (*above*) reveals the site's location on a promontory jutting into Chetumal Bay, with a canal ringing the site on the landward side. Although canoes have not been found at Cerros, murals such as the one from Chichen Itza (*below left*) lend credence to the idea that they were the common form of transport in coastal waters.

remodellings. There are also architectural indications that there were separate work areas in the substructural fill, suggesting to the archaeologists that different work crews were assigned specific areas to "fill in;" clearly, large amounts of labor were required to construct these buildings. The symbolic designs on the stucco masks have been interpreted on the basis of analogies to deities and symbols identified at the time of the Conquest and also in the surviving Maya codices.

Although the bay upon whose shores Cerros now sits is a fairly choppy body of water, the archaeological discovery of certain plant and fish remains at the site indicates that, in the Late Preclassic, Cerros lay on the shores of a calm lagoon. The linear construction jutting out into the lagoon has been interpreted as a jetty or dock. This evidence, together with Cerros's location near the mouth of the New River, has formed the basis for the interpretation that the town was an important trading center.

Many exotic trade materials have been found at Cerros. Analysis of the ceramics also indicates that the town had widespread contacts and that its potters were familiar with the forms and designs of pottery from the Northern Lowlands, other sites in the Southern Lowlands to the east and southeast, and the southern Maya Highlands. Numerous trace-element analyses of obsidian and jade from lowland sites show that their sources were in the Highlands of Guatemala, while Late Postclassic trading patterns of such perishables as salt – which was collected on the coasts of Northern Yucatan – have been projected back to the Late Preclassic in the interpretations of trade at Cerros. By this means the important contemporaneous northern site of Komchen has been interpreted as a trading partner of Cerros. Although no canoes have been found at the site, there are depictions of canoes in Classic art from the Southern Lowlands and it is thought that they would have provided the common form of transport at Cerros for both people and commodities.

The symbolism employed on the stucco masks shows that the town's inhabitants knew of the developing high art styles at major centers in the Southern Maya Lowlands like Lamanai and Tikal, so that the interpretation of Cerros as a trading center goes beyond the location and presence of traded goods. Given the rapid changes at the town – the lack of any local tradition of the forms or symbols at the site, and the introduction of new ceramic forms and styles, as well as an iconographic symbolism – the interpretation of trading contacts being responsible for these introductions is reasonable. The final reports of the Cerros research, currently being published, will hopefully delineate the exact nature of the trade at the town, and its organization. For example, analysis of the residences of elites and non-elites may offer data on differential access to exotics, while comparisons between pre- and post-50 BC houses and house-complexes may enable interpretations to be made of changing economic and social patterns at the site after its florescence. Comparisons with features at ethnohistorically known trading centers such as Cozumel may further help to elucidate trading patterns at Cerros.

Palenque

Most of the basis for this vignette is derived from the architecture of the Temple of the Inscriptions and the great tomb found inside it by the archaeologist Alberto Ruz. Recent advances in the decipherment of the hieroglyphic inscriptions at Palenque, particularly by the noted epigrapher Linda Schele, were also taken into account. The main

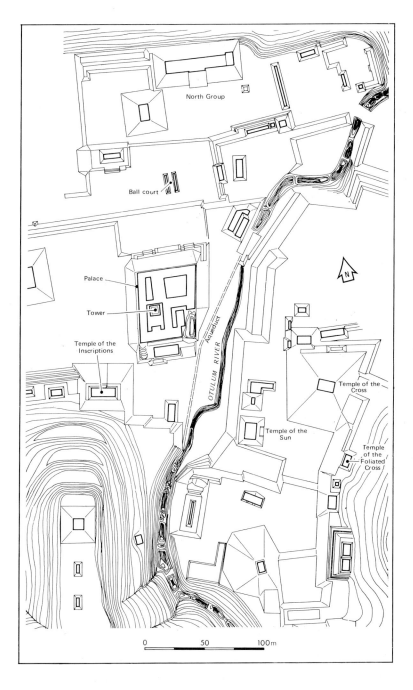

North Group

Ball court

Palace

Tower

Temple of the
Inscriptions

Aqueduct

OTULUM RIVER

Temple of the
Cross

Temple of the
Sun

Temple
of the
Foliated
Cross

N

0   50   100 m

134 **Palenque** Plan of the center.

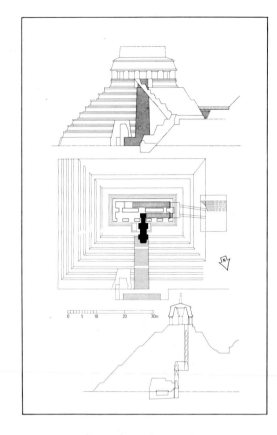

135,136 **Palenque: The Temple of the Inscriptions** General view (*below*) and elevation, plan, and section (*left*) showing Pacal's tomb beneath the building and the vaulted stairway leading to it. See also ill. 52.

character, however, is clearly fictional, because although many of the major architectural triumphs of the ancient Maya show much planning, as do the overall layouts of some cities (such as Uxmal), there is no archaeological evidence that architecture existed as an occupational specialty. Whether or not the rulers planned their monuments must also remain an open question at present.

The name of the great ruler buried inside the Temple of the Inscriptions has been read as Pacal. He founded the first ruling dynasty at Palenque with his accession in AD 615. According to the inscriptions, he was born in AD 603 and died in 684. There has, however, been some dispute over whether the skeletal data agrees with the epigraphic data.

The end of Pacal's reign did not herald the end of Palenque's greatness, for the glyphs indicate that Pacal's successors ruled the city for nearly a century or more, extending the site's influence and power. They also built many of Palenque's most famous buildings, and expanded the central zone to the boundaries we view today.

The inference that Pacal's tomb was planned before the Temple above it is clearly confirmed by the engineering of the structure, while the inference that it was built before Pacal's death is supported by the indications that Pacal's burial was a primary one, that is, his body was placed in its sarcophagus soon after death and was not first buried somewhere else and brought to the tomb later. Moreover, recent research on the sculpture and hieroglyphs of the Temple of the Inscriptions, as well as on its construction, by Linda Schele, has led her to the conclusion – based on the deciphered dates and the content of the inscriptions – that it took about fifteen years to build the temple. The relatively sloppy workmanship on the late inscriptions on Pacal's sarcophagus and tomb has further convinced her that Pacal's death came unexpectedly, and that engineers had to work hurriedly to finish the tomb in time for his funeral. One of the last sculptural additions to the Temple of the Inscriptions before its completion reveals that, 132 days after Pacal's death, one of his sons, Chan Bahlum, ascended to power as the new ruler of Palenque.

The Palenque vignette is a good example of how, by combining glyphic and archaeological data, archaeologists can build a more complete picture of the past.

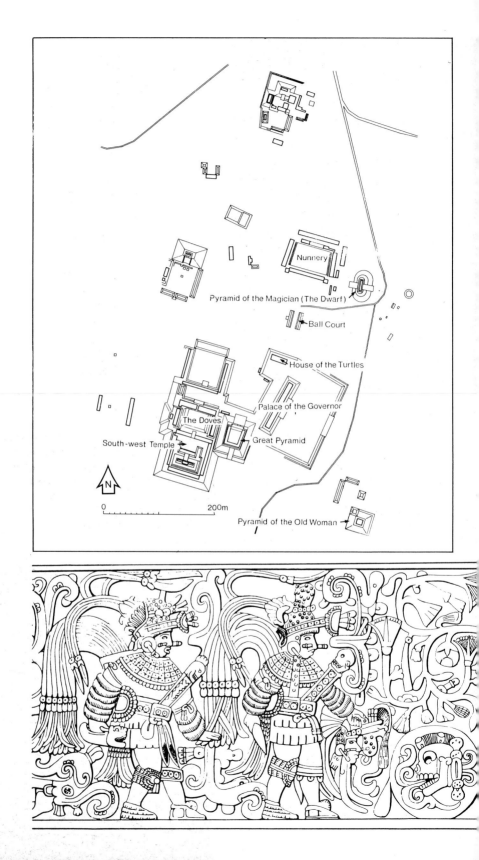

Nunnery

Pyramid of the Magician (The Dwarf)

Ball Court

House of the Turtles

Palace of the Governor

The Doves

South-west Temple

Great Pyramid

N

0   200m

Pyramid of the Old Woman

Uxmal and the ball game

137–141 The presence of a ball court at Uxmal (*left*) indicates that the ball game was played here by the Maya. But details about the game have to be inferred from other sites. A relief carving from Chichen Itza (*below left*) shows members of a victorious team sacrificing their opponents. Equipment worn by the players included yokes and *palmas* (stone versions of each respectively *below right* and *above left*), with the *palma* apparently inserted into the yoke at waist level. Precisely how the game was played, however, or how ball-court markers (*above right*, from Teotihuacan) were used, is not fully understood.

Uxmal

Although some of the finest architectural achievements in the Precolumbian world can be found at the archaeological sites of the hilly Puuc region in the Northern Maya Lowlands, surprisingly little data about the nature of ancient life at these sites is available. At Uxmal, for instance, if you take a few steps away from the great buildings at the core of the site, knowledge about settlement, let alone lifeways, drops precipitously. Except for a highly useful, but small-scale settlement study by the archaeologist Alfredo Barrera Rubio, there is not even a map available for the overall city. The only way to attempt to characterize the settlement at Uxmal, therefore, is to project onto it data from Sayil, where the first full-scale, intensive mapping program at a Puuc region site has been undertaken.

Much more, however, is known about the ancient ball game played at Uxmal and at other cities throughout the Mesoamerican world. Six different lines of evidence exist that can be used in assigning meaning to the ball court at Uxmal. The first is the architecture and layout of the ball court itself. Second is the information from Conquest descriptions of the ball game. Third is a mythical account of the ball game contained in a native Highland Maya document, the *Popul Vuh*, that survived the Conquest. Fourth are illustrations of the ball game, ball courts, and ball players on painted pottery, murals, figurines, and carved monuments. Fifth are material remains from archaeological contexts that can be associated with the ball game, such as yokes that depictions show worn on the hips, probably as protective guards or padding. And sixth is glyphic information from the inscriptions, such as the one on the stone ball court marker at Uxmal. Although we still do not know the exact rules under which the game was played, the reconstruction presented earlier does have a reasonable inferential foundation.

A recent synthesis of the pictorial aspects of the game in the ancient Maya world by Linda Schele and art historian Mary Miller emphasizes the religious and symbolic importance of the game and provides new insight into the violence and death associated with it. They argue that the ball game was a metaphor for battle, and that at the conclusion of some games, captives were sacrificed and their bound bodies rolled down flights of steps from the tops of nearby structures. They, and other scholars such as Michael Coe, also see close metaphorical links between the ball games of the Maya and the ball game of the Hero Twins and the Lords of the Underworld described in the *Popul Vuh*.

They assert that ball games ritually reenacted the age-old conflict between the forces of good and evil.

However, as research by archaeologist Robert Santley and his colleagues indicates, the game also had economic and political significance; much gambling and competition, at least in Aztec times, between the rulers of different urban centers, was acted out through the game. Some caution must also be exercised in not taking scenes on decorated pottery or sculpture too literally in interpreting ancient Maya culture. Events may sometimes have been exaggerated for better effect.

Tula

The Toltecs are one of the best-known civilizations in American archaeology, yet surprisingly little is known about them archaeologically. Although historical materials from the time of the Spanish Conquest frequently mention the Toltecs, the gap between their heyday in the eleventh and twelfth centuries and the sixteenth-century Spanish Conquest was large enough to shroud them in a confusing mix of history and mythology. Moreover, the Aztecs, who portrayed themselves as the direct successors to the achievements of the powerful Toltecs, rewrote history so as to glorify their putative ancestors. Many Toltec monuments were removed from their original locations and brought to the Aztec capital of Tenochtitlan, thus making it difficult to assess the original Toltec sites.

In recent years, however, the clouds have begun to lift to give us a clearer picture of the Toltecs. More than four decades ago, on the basis of ethnohistoric documents describing Tula and an examination of sites in a pre-Aztec time horizon that fit these descriptions, the historian Wigberto Jimenez Moreno, and the archaeologist Jorge Acosta, were able to argue convincingly that the site of Tula in the modern Mexican state of Hidalgo was ancient Tollan, capital of the Toltecs. First Acosta, and then more recently Richard Diehl and Eduardo Matos Moctezuma, have undertaken extensive excavations and surveys at Tula. It is on their reports that the Tula vignette is based.

Research has revealed the nature of Toltec residential groupings, showing a somewhat haphazard, agglutinated layout of residential clusters with little evidence of the careful planning previously seen at Teotihuacan. A variety of courtyards and alleys with houses and storage rooms built one next to the other have been discovered.

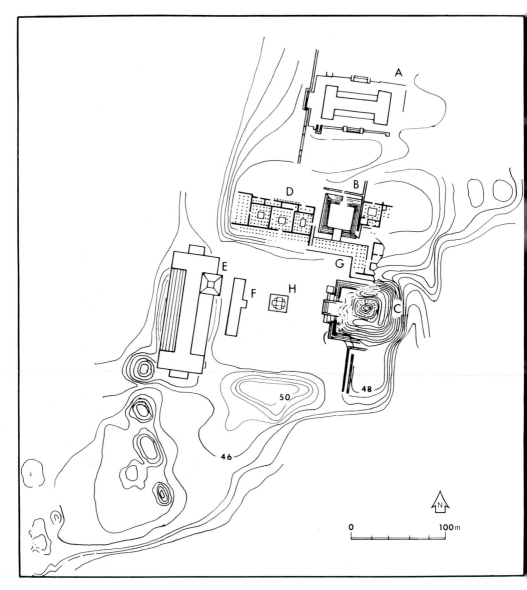

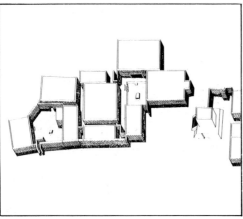

142,143 **Tula** The central area of Tula (known as Tula Grande), with its two pyramids (B,C), two ball courts (A,E), palace (D) and other structures, is the most famous part of the site. But recent excavations nearby have revealed the actual dwellings of the inhabitants. They lived in somewhat haphazard clusters of houses (*left*), with courtyards, storage rooms, and alleys separating them.

Locations where it is hypothesized that different manufacturing activities took place have been identified. These include areas for ceramic manufacture and obsidian tool production. Molds for figurines have also been found in a variety of domestic contexts, indicating another craft specialty, and in addition, a number of artifacts identified as spindle whorls have been excavated, leading to the inference that cotton weaving was another important occupation. Fractured pieces of stone bowls, from which it has been possible to analyze the various stages of stone bowl production, have been discovered throughout the site, but the manufacturing locales for these vessels, found exclusively in elite contexts, have yet to be uncovered.

In one excavation, Diehl found a cache of pottery vessels with several pots from Central America; he cited this as evidence for trading contacts between this area and the Toltecs. Traders might have taken either overland routes, or sea routes along the Pacific coast. Based on the distribution of Toltec or Toltec-influenced goods throughout Mexico and adjacent areas, and the presence of exotic items at Tula, there is good reason to believe that Tula had widespread contacts throughout ancient Mexico into the frontier areas to both the north and south. Further research, including the sourcing and distribution of various artifacts, would give a more detailed picture of Toltec trade.

While the military prowess of the Toltecs may have been exaggerated by the Aztecs, depictions of military symbols and death abound at Tula. Just what role the military played in the life of Tula and its expansion is nevertheless little understood. Many scholars have noted that the extent of the later Aztec empire, let alone its nature, would be exceedingly difficult to delineate on the basis of archaeological evidence alone. Without the historical materials from the Conquest Period, it is quite possible that archaeologists might significantly misjudge the political and economic spread of the Aztecs, given the current means of interpreting the archaeological record. If such is the case with the Aztecs, then it must be even more so for the Toltecs, about whom we know much less.

In order to understand better the role of the military at Tula and the part it played in Toltec expansion, it may be helpful, therefore, to use the historical data about the Aztecs and try to link specific aspects of Aztec militarism with material patterns in the archaeological record. If such links could be found, archaeologists would be in a position to expand the analogy to the earlier Toltec time horizon. This is just one of many examples where the use of both archaeological and historical

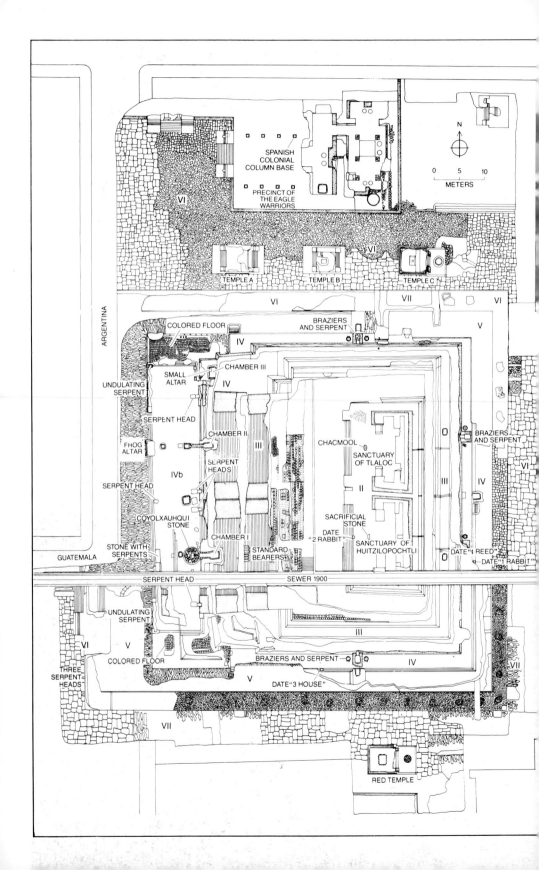

SPANISH
COLONIAL
COLUMN BASE

PRECINCT OF
THE EAGLE
WARRIORS

VI

N

0   5   10
METERS

VI

TEMPLE A   TEMPLE B   TEMPLE C

VI   VII   VI

ARGENTINA

COLORED FLOOR   BRAZIERS
AND SERPENT

IV   V

CHAMBER III

UNDULATING
SERPENT

SMALL
ALTAR

SERPENT HEAD   IV

CHAMBER II   BRAZIERS
AND SERPENT

FHOG
ALTAR   III   CHACMOOL   SANCTUARY
OF TLALOC   VI

IVb   SERPENT
HEADS   II   III   IV

SERPENT HEAD

COYOLXAUHQUI
STONE   SACRIFICIAL
STONE

STONE WITH   CHAMBER I   DATE   SANCTUARY OF
SERPENTS   "2 RABBIT"   HUITZILOPOCHTLI

GUATEMALA   STANDARD   DATE"1 REED"
BEARERS   DATE"1 RABBIT"

SERPENT HEAD   SEWER 1900

UNDULATING
SERPENT   III

VI   V   COLORED FLOOR   BRAZIERS AND SERPENT   IV   VII

THREE
SERPENT
HEADS   V   DATE"3 HOUSE"

VII

RED TEMPLE

The Great Temple of Tenochtitlan

144–146 The Great Temple excavations (1978–1982) unearthed a giant pyramidal platform rebuilt at least six times before its destruction by the Spaniards. The plan (*left*) shows the location of many of the remarkable structures and finds, including the Eagle Warrior precinct with its life-size effigy (*above*). Chamber III, with a rich offering of polychrome jars and stone masks (*below*), was placed just below Cache 48 containing the skeletons of more than forty children. Dedicated to Tlaloc the rain god, both offerings were buried during the later part of the reign of Moctezuma I (1440–1469).

information, or the collaboration between archaeologists and ethno-historians, might improve and strengthen archaeological analogies.

Tenochtitlan

The vignette on the *chinampa* worker living to the south of Tenochtitlan differs from all the others in this book in that it is based on historic data, supplemented by ethnographic information about the surviving *chinampa* zone in Xochimilco, rather than on archaeological investigation – although it can be linked to the archaeological record in some aspects.

Most scholarly understandings of the Aztecs are based on the historic record. This may be because the focus of Aztec civilization, the city of Tenochtitlan, as well as surrounding centers, were either destroyed by the Spaniards or have been covered over by the huge urban metropolis of Mexico City, so that archaeologists have not been attracted by this civilization as much as they have been by earlier ones. Except for the serendipitous discoveries of Aztec materials, such as those uncovered when Mexico City's subway was excavated, or the recent, spectacular unearthing of part of the *Templo Mayor* (Great Temple) in the downtown sector of Mexico City, it has been nearly impossible to excavate Tenochtitlan. Moreover, the rich historical database, which includes native documents, eyewitness accounts of the Conquest, descriptions of New Spain by the first wave of Spaniards immediately after the Conquest, and a variety of legal documents particularly about land disputes, appears to have discouraged archaeological research.

There are two reasons, however, why a broader archaeological contribution would be of value in increasing our understanding of the Aztec civilization. One is that historical records plainly cannot provide all the details about various aspects of Aztec culture and development that scholars might wish to know. The research by archaeologist Eduardo Matos Moctezuma at the Templo Mayor, shows how archaeological and historic data, when used in tandem, can amplify each other to give scholars a much fuller picture than either line of evidence could have provided on its own. Let me cite two examples of this. First, Matos's excavations revealed a series of early rebuildings of the temple, with changes and new additions at each stage, while the historical sources provided information about the nature of the rituals associated with the structure, such as the huge number of sacrifices made in AD 1487 at the dedication of the temple and the significance of the deities whose statues the excavators uncovered. Second, a large quantity of stone jars bearing representations of Tlaloc, the rain god, were found in the excavations. Underneath eleven of these vessels (in Cache 48), Matos discovered a number of infant burials. On the basis of information in the writings of the Spanish cleric Sahagún, Matos was able to link these burials to the practice of infant sacrifice to Tlaloc on certain religious occasions.

The second reason as to why archaeology is valid in an historical situation reiterates a point made above in the discussion of the Toltecs, namely, that excavations at Aztec sites (apart from Tenochtitlan) where there are historical controls may help to provide links between aspects of their state expansion – political, economic, or military – and the archaeological record. If the environmental parameters could then be controlled – what archaeologists usually mean when they say "all things being equal" – then it might be possible to generalize such links to other situations. A spate of new research by scholars such as Elizabeth Brumfiel, Mary Hodge, and Michael Smith is highly promising in this regard.

Summary

Two points should be obvious from our discussion of the analogical backgrounds of the vignettes presented earlier. First, the number of close analogies is surprisingly slim. Second, archaeologists know more about elite activities in the past than non-elite ones. What can be done to rectify these problems? Attempts have been made to deal with the second one since the end of World War II, when archaeology widened its perspective beyond the spectacular remains to include the more mundane traces of peasant farmers and middle class artisans. The first problem is clearly more difficult. It is not a question that just affects scholars concerned with ancient Mexico; it is arguably one of the most critical issues facing archaeologists today.

How can my "just-so stories" be made more reliable and secure? Certainly, they are not just fabricated; there are many points in the vignettes that are linked with inferential clues derived from archaeo-logical research. The most dependable parts of the vignettes are those where plausible links can be made between the material archaeo-logical record and historic accounts, such as is the case with the ancient ball game. But what about the vast majority of situations where an historical link cannot be made? In these cases, historical or modern ethnographic data from the general Mexican area can still be of great use, particularly where the environment – including topography, climate, plant and animal availability, and access to mineral resources – are deemed to be more or less constant.

Most archaeological field projects in Mexico today have ethno-archaeological and/or ethnohistoric components so that interpretation of the archaeological record goes hand in hand with the fieldwork. Moreover, an increasing number of scholars are becoming aware that terms such as "market" or "craft production area" that they have blithely used in the past to stipulate the meanings of part of the archaeological record – "this wide open area is a market" or "this concentration of obsidian flakes is a workshop" – must be linked with material signatures that can be identified archaeologically.

As the scope of archaeological research expands with surveys so that not only the rural areas around urban centers are explored but also the zones between sites; as excavation strategies improve with more horizontal excavation of domestic areas instead of small test pits (what Kent Flannery has labeled "telephone booths"); and as recovery methods in excavations improve and analytic techniques offering new information about the details of everyday life are utilized, so scholars will have larger and better controlled amounts of data available for interpretation. With more self-conscious concern for the analogies needed to give meaning to these data now awakening in the discipline, I am optimistic that it will soon be feasible to offer more secure, richer answers to that ubiquitous query, "What was it like?".

Gazetteer

I have only had opportunity in the above pages to discuss some of the best-known urban centers of Precolumbian Mesoamerica. Yet urban development, particularly after the time of Christ, was not limited to just a few sites. Hundreds of probable cities have been identified, but many are known only superficially at best; most lack detailed settlement maps, so that without new field research it is difficult to decide whether or not they were cities. In some cases, historic and modern urban growth has made it all but impossible to conduct field research today; we have little or no direct archaeological information for many of the cities recorded by the sixteenth-century Spaniards.

I list below fifty selected examples for which we do have some archaeological and/or historical knowledge. Settlement data are patchy, but where available, I have made some mention of them. A reference is given for each city to provide a starting point for those readers who wish for more detailed information. Twenty of the sites have been starred (*): these hold the most interest for tourists and are reasonably accessible. A few additional sentences about the locations of these twenty sites have been added to the brief discussions that follow; specific guidebooks for many of them can be obtained from the Mexican Government and further information may also be found in Joyce Kelly's *The Complete Visitor's Guide to Mesoamerica* (University of Oklahoma Press, Norman, 1982), and *An Archaeological Guide to Mexico's Yucatan Peninsula* (University of Oklahoma Press, Norman, 1993).

Sites are keyed to map of Mesoamerica

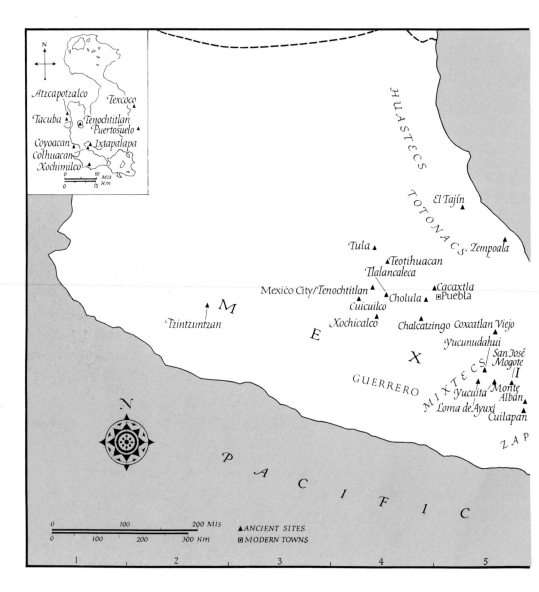

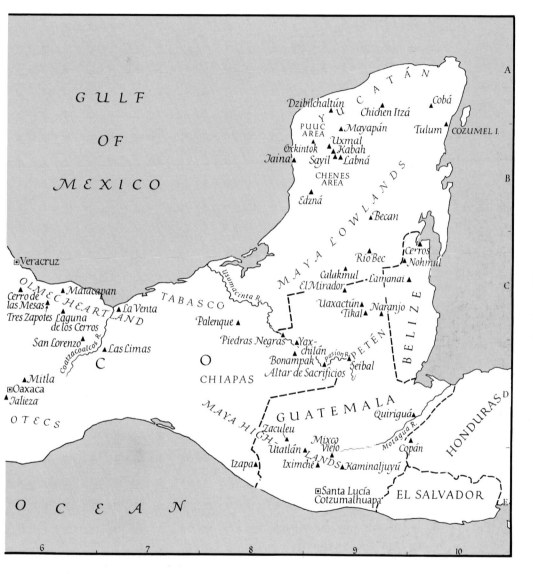

147 Map of Mesoamerica, showing sites mentioned in the text and gazetteer.

Azcapotzalco (A1)

This Basin of Mexico site was one of the largest cities (apart from Tenochtitlan) during the fifteenth and early sixteenth centuries AD. Although it is known from historical writings, the modern urban expansion of Mexico City has made archaeological research on this important political and economic center almost impossible. Coyoacan, Ixtapalapa, Tacuba, and Xochimilco were other important contemporary cities in the Basin of Mexico.

Reference: William T. Sanders, Jeffrey R. Parsons, and Robert S. Santley, *The Basin of Mexico: Ecological Processes in the Evolution of a Civilization* (Academic Press, New York, 1979).

Becan (B9)

Becan is located in the Central Maya Lowlands in the Rio Bec region. Recent research by Tulane University has revealed an occupational sequence from Middle Preclassic to Terminal Classic times. Becan is best known for the massive earthen rampart and ditch (some 16 m wide and 5 m deep) that was built in the Late Preclassic Period, and for its large buildings in the distinctive Rio Bec architectural style, dating to the site's Late Classic florescence.

Reference: Prentice M. Thomas, Jr, *Prehistoric Maya Settlement Patterns at Becan, Campeche, Mexico* (Middle American Research Institute, Tulane University, Publication 45, New Orleans 1981).

Calakmul (C9)

Calakmul is a huge Classic Maya city located at the northern extreme of the southern Lowlands. It is renowned for its vast number of stelae and also for its role as a major regional capital, according to an interpretation made by the archaeologist Joyce Marcus and others. On-going research at the site indicates that it is much more extensive than previously thought.

Reference: William J. Folan, "Calakmul, Campeche: A Centralized Urban Administrative Center in the Northern Peten," *World Archaeology*, Vol. 24, No. 1 (1992): 158–168.

Cerros (C10)

Located in the Southern Maya Lowlands on the shore of Chetumal Bay in Northern Belize. Recent excavations by Southern Methodist University have revealed that the site reached its height well before the beginning of the Classic Period (during the Late Preclassic Period, just before the time of Christ), and was an important trading center of its day. A large temple with beautiful stucco masks flanking a central stairway is the building for which it is best known. See Chapters Five and Twelve for further details and a site plan.

Reference: Robin A. Robertson and David A. Freidel (eds), *Archaeology at Cerros, Belize, Central America, Vol. I: An Interim Report* (Southern Methodist University Press, Dallas, 1986).

*Chichen Itza (A9)

One of the best-known of the Maya cities. Readily accessible by car or bus (Merida Central Bus Station) on Highway 180 from either Merida (110 km) or the resort area of Cancun on the east coast of the Yucatan Peninsula (200 km), it is at its most magnificent in the Spring. Look for signposting near the town of Piste. Hotels and other facilities are adjacent to the site and there is a sound and light show in the evenings.

Chichen Itza is situated in the center of the Northern Lowlands. It has a long sequence but its height can be placed at about

148 The great ball court at Chichen Itza.

AD 800–1100. It continued to play a role as an important pilgrimage shrine well into the sixteenth century. While no full, intensive settlement mapping of the site has ever been undertaken, on-going research is finally providing a picture of the nature and extent of Chichen Itza's urban core. It is most famous for its sacred well (or *cenote*) and for its many buildings, such as the Castillo and the Temple of the Warriors, which show "Mexican" influences that some scholars have interpreted as evidence of a Toltec conquest of the site and others have seen as Putun or Mexicanized Maya influence.

Reference: Clemency Chase Coggins and Orrin C. Shane III (eds) *Cenote of Sacrifice: Maya Treasures from the Sacred Well at Chichen Itza* (University of Texas Press, Austin, 1984).

* Cholula (C4)

This site, which looks equally impressive in all seasons, lies about 13 km west of the city of Puebla, along Highway 190, and is accessible by car or bus. The approach is clearly signposted.

Cholula has what is probably the biggest pyramid in Mesoamerica, although much of the structure's base is a natural hill and the amount of human construction is unclear. The site flourished throughout the Classic Period, particularly in the Terminal Classic after the decline of Teotihuacan in the eighth century AD, and into the Early Postclassic when its great pyramid may have been completed. It was still a sizeable city at the time of the Spanish Conquest.

Reference: Ignacio Marquina (ed.), *Proyecto Cholula* (Serie Investigaciones, Instituto Nacional de Antropología e Historia, Vol. 19, Mexico, 1970).

* Coba (A10)

A paved road makes this site accessible by car from either Merida (146 km) or Cancun. The road is clearly marked and cuts off from Highway 180 at Nuevo X-Can, or from Highway 307 just south of Tulum. A hotel and other facilities serve the site which is best visited in the Spring.

Coba is a large city located on the eastern edge of the Northern Maya Lowlands. Recent research by North American and Mexican scholars has shown that, although the site had a major Late Classic florescence, it continued to play an important political role into the Terminal Classic and Early Postclassic Periods. A long causeway (or *sacbe*) links Coba with the site of Yaxuna which lies to the south of Chichen Itza in the central Northern Lowlands.

Reference: C. Antonio Benevides, *Coba: Una ciudad prehispanica de Quintana Rio* (Instituto Nacional de Antropología e Historia, Mexico, 1981).

* Copan (D10)

This Honduran site can be reached by airplane or by paved road from San Pedro Sula (200 km). Take route CA4 to Santa Rosa de Copan and then route CA11 to the town of Copan where the nearby site is clearly signposted. Hotels and other facilities are available in the town.

Copan is the southernmost of the great Lowland Maya sites and during its Late Classic heyday was the largest of them. It is particularly famous for its plentiful and finely carved monuments and sculpture. Decipherment of some of its hieroglyphic inscriptions has revealed a dynastic sequence of rulers at the site, while recent and on-going research by a variety of institutions has provided details of the settlement expansion of the Copan Valley.

Reference: William L. Fash, *Scribes, Warriors, and Kings: The City of Copan and the Ancient Maya* (Thames and Hudson, London and New York, 1991).

Coxcatlan Viejo (C5)

Coxcatlan Viejo lies in the Tehuacan Valley of southern Puebla. It is situated on a series of ridges, with plazas on top of each ridge, and a particularly large plaza area located at the foot of the ridges. The hillsides too are terraced. In total, the site occupies about 1 sq km. Numerous manufacturing areas, particularly for ceramics, were found by a recent R.S. Peabody Foundation project. The site dates mainly to the Late Postclassic Period.

Reference: Edward B. Sisson, *First Annual Report of the Coxcatlan Project* (Robert S. Peabody Foundation for Archaeology, Andover, Mass., 1973).

Cuicuilco (C4)

Located in the southwest corner of the Valley of Mexico. By the beginning of the first millennium BC, Cuicuilco was growing in size and population. By 300 BC it was probably the largest center in the Valley, and was almost certainly urban, yet soon thereafter it was eclipsed by Teotihuacan and went into decline. Whether its demise was a direct consequence of volcanic eruptions that covered nearby agricultural lands with lava is a matter of dispute. Cuicuilco's best-known building is an immense round, multi-level structure.

Reference: William T. Sanders, Jeffrey R. Parsons, and Robert S. Santley, *The Basin of Mexico: Ecological Processes in the Evolution of a Civilization* (Academic Press, New York, 1979).

* Dzibilchaltun (A9)

Accessible by car or bus from Merida in about half an hour's driving time. Take Highway 261 toward Progresso and look out for signposting to the site after 14 km; 7 km down this road Dzibilchaltun is signposted again. Facilities are available at the site.

Dzibilchaltun was a major urban center in the Northern Maya Lowlands with a very long sequence from the Middle Preclassic through to the Spanish Conquest. Intensive research by Tulane University has shown that the site had an extensive, heavily populated settlement zone and that it had reached urban proportions by Classic times. This research also revealed strong cultural continuities throughout the Classic into the Postclassic Period.

Reference: E. Wyllys Andrews IV and E. Wyllys Andrews V, *Excavations at Dzibilchaltun, Yucatan, Mexico* (Middle American Research Institute, Tulane University, Publication 48, New Orleans, 1980).

* Edzna (B9)

This site is in the state of Campeche on Highway 188 (just off Highway 261). It is well signposted and can be reached by paved road (a full day's outing) from Merida (200 km) or from Campeche City (65 km). Limited facilities are available at the site.

Edzna is situated on the southwestern side of the Northern Maya Lowlands. During the Late Classic Period the site reached urban proportions. Recent research by Brigham Young University has revealed a large canal system that was probably part of an intensive agricultural development supporting the city. Edzna is particularly famous for its five-storey "palace" at the center of the site.

Reference: Ray T. Matheny, Deane L. Gurr, Donald W. Forsyth, and F. Richard Hauck, *Investigations at Edzna, Campeche, Mexico* (Papers of the New World Archaeological Foundation, Brigham Young University, No. 46, Provo, 1983).

El Mirador (C9)

Located in the northern reaches of the Southern Maya Lowlands, this site was first reported on by the archaeologist Ian Graham in the 1960s. New research by several institutions, especially Brigham Young University, has revealed a great Late Preclassic florescence, including a monumental architectural complex that is the largest construction of the time in the Maya area. El Mirador is one of the earliest urban centers in the Lowlands and is contemporary with, and larger than, similar developments at Cerros, Cuello, Lamanai, and Tikal.

Reference: Ray Matheny, "Investigations at El Mirador, Peten, Guatemala," *National Geographic Research*, Vol. 2, (1986):332–353.

* El Tajin (B5)

Located south of the town of Papantla (24 km east of Poza Rica) in the state of Veracruz. It is signposted just off Highway 180 and can be reached by paved road. El Tajin looks impressive in any season. Facilities are available at the site.

El Tajin is situated in northern Veracruz in the Gulf Coast region. The site is famous for its architecture (including the well-known Pyramid of the Niches), sculpture, and ball courts. The lack of intensive settlement research or recent publications on chronology make it difficult to characterize El Tajin in relation to size and growth. The principal architecture dates to Classic times with the site's florescence possibly dating to the time of the decline of Teotihuacan, and into the Early Postclassic Period.

Reference: José García Payon, *El Tajin: Official Guide* (Instituto Nacional de Antropología e Historia, Mexico, 1957).

* Iximche (E9)

This site in the Guatemalan Highlands can be reached by car (or by the bus for Tecpan) from Guatemala City in about an hour and a half's driving time, going west along Highway 1. There is a short stretch of dirt road from Tecpan to Iximche which lies to the south of this town. The time of year will not affect your visit.

Iximche is located south of Utatlan. It was the capital of the Cakchiquel, a Maya group which broke away from the control of the Quiche about A D 1470. Iximche served as the base for Cakchiquel expansion during the fifty or so years of its existence. It is situated on a 1-km-long and 200–400-m-wide plateau. The center is divided into two zones, one probably civic in function, the other residential. A moat separates the two.

Reference: John W. Fox, *Quiche Conquest* (University of New Mexico Press, Albuquerque, 1978).

Ixtapalapa (B1)

See information on Azcapotzalco, which also applies to this site.

Reference: Richard E. Blanton, *Prehispanic Settlement Patterns of the Ixtapalapa Peninsula Region, Mexico* (Occasional Papers in Anthropology, The Pennsylvania State University, No. 6, University Park, 1972).

Izapa (E8)

Located in the piedmont of Chiapas near the Pacific Ocean and just west of the Mexican-Guatemalan border. Research by the New World Archaeological Foundation has revealed a lengthy sequence that stretches from the Early Preclassic to the Early Postclassic. The most famous phase, however, dates from 300 BC to 50 BC, when a series of sculptures and monuments were carved with early hieroglyphc (calendric) inscriptions and figures in the "Izapan" style. The site at this time covered more than 3.5 sq. km, and had many massive platforms and buildings.

Reference: Gareth W. Lowe, Thomas A. Lee, Jr, and Eduardo Martinez Espinosa, *Izapa: An Introduction to the Ruins and Monuments* (Papers of the New World Archaeological Foundation, Brigham Young University, No. 31, Provo, 1982).

Jalieza (D6)

Jalieza is located in the piedmont zone of the Valle Grande arm of the Valley of Oaxaca. It reached its height during the Early Classic, from AD 250 to 450. This important city covered over 4 sq. km and had about 12,000 inhabitants living on at least 700 residential terraces. Jalieza appears to have been a regional political and economic center that was subordinate to Monte Alban. Interestingly, for a site of its size, it has relatively little large-scale architecture.

Reference: Richard E. Blanton and Stephen A. Kowalewski, "Monte Alban and After in the Valley of Oxcaca," in Victoria R. Bricker (gen. ed.) and Jeremy A. Sabloff (vol. ed.), *Supplement to the Handbook of Middle American Indians*, Vol. 1, pp. 94–116 (University of Texas Press, Austin, 1981).

Kaminaljuyu (E9)

This Maya site is situated within the boundaries of modern-day Guatemala City in the southern Guatemalan Highlands. Founded in the Preclassic Period, Kaminaljuyu is best known for its Early Classic florescence which shows strong Teotihuacan influence in architecture, ceramics, and non-ceramic artifacts. Some have argued that Kaminaljuyu was conquered by Teotihuacan to secure control of the nearby obsidian source, and trade routes to the Pacific Lowlands. Research by Pennsylvania State University has detailed a long settlement sequence.

Reference: J.W. Michels (ed.) *Settlement Pattern Excavations at Kaminaljuyu, Guatemala* (Pennsylvania State University Press Monograph Series on Kaminaljuyu, University Park, 1979).

Lamanai (C10)

Located on the New River in Belize, this Southern Maya Lowland site had a very long sequence, from 800 BC until after the Spanish Conquest in the sixteenth century AD. On-going research by the Royal Ontario Museum has revealed large-scale construction in the Late Classic Period, as well as a relatively rare continuity from Classic to Postclassic times.

Reference: David Pendergast, "Lamanai, Belize: Summary of Excavation Results, 1974–1980," *Journal of Field Archaeology*, Vol. 8, No. 1 (1981):29–53.

Loma de Ayuxi (Yanhuitlan, D5)

Loma de Ayuxi was one of many Late Postclassic cities in the Mixteca. It was probably the capital of the powerful kingdom of Yanhuitlan and occupied an area of more than 1 sq. km. The site has a ceremonial precinct and a large central elite residence, or "palace" complex. Many sites were subject to Yanhuitlan, including Yucuita.

Reference: Ronald Spores, *The Mixtecs in Ancient and Colonial Times* (University of Oklahoma Press, Norman, 1984).

Matacapan (C6)

Matacapan is located in the Tuxtlas region of the southern Gulf Coast. It has a long sequence beginning in Early Preclassic times but is perhaps best known for its Early Classic settlement when it came under the influence of Teotihuacan. A Teotihuacan *barrio*, complete with Central Mexican architecture, has been found there. The site's importance is related in part to its manufacture of obsidian tools. Research by a University of New Mexico–Universidad Veracruzana team has shown that, by Late Classic times, Matacapan covered more than 5.5 sq. km, had numerous obsidian and ceramic workshops, and may have had a population of between 3,000 and 7,000 people.

Reference: Philip J. Arnold III and Robert S. Santley, "Household Ceramic Production at Middle Classic Period Matacapan," in Robert S. Santley and Kenneth G. Hirth (eds.), *Prehispanic Domestic Units in Western Mesoamerica*, pp. 227–248 (CRC Press, Boca Raton, 1993).

* Mayapan (B9)

Signposted near the town of Telchaquillo, this site is accessible by car from Merida (50 km) on a paved road (except for a short dirt-road stretch to get into the site). A bus runs from Merida to Telchaquillo. There are no facilities at the site.

Mayapan was a highly nucleated, walled city located in Northern Yucatan. It succeeded Chichen Itza as the major center of the Northern Maya Lowlands in the mid-thirteenth century. Intensive research by the Carnegie Institution of Washington showed that it flourished for 200 years, reaching a population of 12,000–13,000 people. Mayapan was the capital of a confederacy that covered much of the Northern Lowlands. This confederacy disintegrated when Mayapan declined some decades prior to the arrival of the Spanish.

Reference: H.E.D. Pollock, Ralph L. Roys, T. Proskouriakoff, and A. Ledyard Smith, *Mayapan, Yucatan, Mexico* (Carnegie Institution of Washington, Publication 619, 1962).

* Mitla (D6)

This famous site is easily reached by car or tourist bus from downtown Oaxaca City (43 km), via Highway 190. It is well signposted, and facilities are available at the site. You would have time to visit Monte Alban on the same day.

Mitla has a long history of occupation from the Early Preclassic to the Spanish Conquest. Its greatest expansion, however, was reached in Late Postclassic times. Recent research has shown that the urban core was 1–2 sq. km in size with a surrounding suburban area, while the rural zone where intensive agriculture was practiced may have covered more than 20 sq. km. The best-known buildings at Mitla are the two Zapotec "palaces," with stone mosaic designs on their exteriors.

Reference: Kent V. Flannery and Joyce Marcus, "Urban Mitla and its Rural Hinterland," in Kent Flannery and Joyce Marcus (eds), *The Cloud People*, pp. 295–300 (Academic Press, New York, 1983).

* Monte Alban (D5)

Easily accessible by car or tourist bus from downtown Oaxaca City (2.5 km), along a paved road that runs out of Oaxaca City to the west along the Rio Atoyac. The site is well signposted and facilities are available.

Monte Alban, located in the Valley of Oaxaca, was the capital of the Zapotecs. It was founded around 500 BC and was probably the first true urban center in ancient Mexico. It flourished until AD 700, although it continued to function, particularly as a burial site, until the Spanish Conquest. Even though it is not as visibly organized or as large (its population never exceeded 25,000–30,000 people) as its contemporary, Teotihuacan, it was an important force in the greater Oaxaca region for many centuries. Settlement survey has shown that many of the inhabitants of the city lived on terraces that were built on the hillsides around Monte Alban. Early in its history, the so-called "Danzante" slabs were carved and erected to commemorate Monte Alban's conquests. See Chapters Three and Twelve for further details and a site plan.

Reference: Richard E. Blanton, *Monte Alban: Settlement Patterns at the Ancient Zapotec Capital* (Academic Press, New York, 1978).

Nohmul (C9)

Located in Northern Belize in the Southern Maya Lowlands, Nohmul has recently been investigated by a British/American team. Its long sequence is noted for a strong Terminal Classic occupation that shows ties to the Northern Lowlands and a possible link with the intensive agriculture practiced at nearby Pulltrouser Swamp. The latter has been intensively studied by a combined archaeological/ecological project.

Reference: Norman Hammond, *Nohmul: A Prehistoric Maya Community in Belize, Excavations 1973–1983* (BAR International Series, Oxford, England, 1985).

Oxkintok (B9)

This site is an important Puuc region center in the Northern Maya Lowlands and had its florescence from about AD 800 to 1000. Unlike most other Puuc region sites, it also had an important Early Classic-Late Classic occupation. On-going research by a Spanish archaeological team is revealing more details of this extensive city's archaeological development.

Reference: Miguel Rivera Dorado, "Oxkintok: Resultados de la temporada de 1991," *Mexicon*, Vol. 15, No. 4 (1993): 75–78.

* Palenque (C8)

This Classic Maya site looks particularly impressive in the Spring. Situated 150 km southeast of Villahermosa, capital of the state of Tabasco, it can be reached by car or

149 Palenque: view from the North Group of temples towards the Temple of the Inscriptions (in the distance). The Palace tower is also visible.

bus along Highway 186. The site is well sign-posted, and many hotels are available in the immediate vicinity.

Palenque is located near what was the western frontier of the Lowland Maya realm and reached its height during the Late Classic Period, from AD 600 to 800. It is renowned for its beautiful sculpture; the Temple of the Inscriptions covering the spectacular tomb of the ruler Pacal; and the palace complex with its imposing tower. A full settlement survey of the site has never been published, so it is impossible to know the exact size and extent of the city, or its population. Nevertheless, hieroglyphic and ceramic studies indicate that, during Late Classic times, Palenque was a major center that expanded its influence through warfare and marriage alliances along the drainage of the Usumacinta River. See Chapters Five and Twelve for further details and a site plan.

Reference: Merle Greene Robertson, *The Sculpture of Palenque*, Vol. 1 (Princeton University Press, Princeton, 1983).

Puertosuelo (A2)

Located in the Basin of Mexico. It had a brief but major rise to prominence from AD 750 to 950, after the decline of Teotihuacan. Puertosuelo was highly nucleated and is estimated to have had a population of around 12,000 people. It had a large built-up ceremonial area most of the architecture of which dates to the Terminal Classic Period.

Reference: William T. Sanders, Jeffrey R. Parsons, Robert S. Santley, *The Basin of Mexico: Ecological Processes in the Evolution of a Civilization* (Academic Press, New York, 1979).

* San Gervasio (Cozumel, A10)

If possible, visit this site in the Spring. It is easily reached by car from the town of San Miguel (10 km). The road you should take does not have a number, but you can ask at any hotel for directions.

San Gervasio is the largest site on the Maya island of Cozumel which lies off the East Coast of the Yucatan Peninsula. Cozumel is strategically located along waterborne trade routes from Honduras around the peninsula to the Gulf Coast Lowlands, and was an important trading center in the Late Postclassic Period, from about AD 1250 to the time of the Spanish Conquest. San Gervasio is situated in the northern center of the island. Research by a joint Harvard-Arizona team in the 1970s, and recent research by the Mexican government, has shown that it started to grow in importance around AD 800, reaching its zenith in the fifteenth century. Raised causeways link the site with both the east coast of the island and the lagoons in the north where trading canoes may have landed.

Reference: David A. Freidel and Jeremy A. Sabloff, *Cozumel: Late Maya Settlement Patterns* (Academic Press, New York, 1984).

San Lorenzo (D6)

Located near the Coatzacoalcos River in the Gulf Coast Lowlands of modern-day Veracruz. The rise of ancient Mexico's first civilization, the Olmec, has been clearly traced at San Lorenzo, the best known of the lowland Olmec religious centers. The rich levee lands of the nearby river may have provided the agricultural base that supported the sizeable community. The site was built on an artificially shaped and leveled hilltop – just one of a number of examples of the Olmec leaders' ability to organize the labor of the inhabitants of the site and the surrounding area. San Lorenzo was first settled around 1500 BC and flourished between 1200 and 900 BC. Although it never reached urban proportions, at its height approximately 1,000 people lived in San Lorenzo. It is particularly famous for its great carved stone heads, perhaps portraits of its rulers, and the channeling of water for use in religious ceremonies of the day.

Reference: Michael D. Coe and Richard Diehl, *In the Land of the Olmec: The Archaeology of San Lorenzo, Tenochtitlan* (University of Texas Press, Austin, 1980).

* Sayil (B9)

Located about half an hour's drive south of Uxmal. It is well signposted and can easily be reached by car on a paved road. There is no bus. Facilities are available at the site.

Sayil is situated in the Puuc region of the Northern Maya Lowlands. Settlement research by a University of Pittsburgh–University of New Mexico team has shown that the urban center covered some 5 sq. km during the site's florescence, from AD 700 to 900. Numerous underground cisterns (or *chultuns*), which captured rainwater during the wet season, provided water for the populace during the dry season.

Reference: Jeremy A. Sabloff and Gair Tourtellot, *The Ancient Maya City of Sayil: The Mapping of a Puuc Region Center* (Middle American Research Institute, Tulane University, Publication 60, New Orleans, 1991).

Seibal (D9)

Located on a hill overlooking the Pasion River in the Southern Maya Lowlands, Seibal flourished briefly but significantly between AD 770 and 900, at a time when most other Southern Lowlands sites were declining in population and importance. Recent research by the Peabody Museum, Harvard University, has shown that Seibal was founded before 800 BC. Its late development was stimulated by a takeover of the site by non-Classic Maya intruders – often termed Putun – from the Gulf Coast Lowlands.

Reference: Gordon R. Willey, A. Ledyard Smith, Gair Tourtellot III, and Ian Graham, *Excavations at Seibal, Introduction: The Site and Its Setting* (Memoirs of the Peabody Museum, Harvard University, Vol. 13, No. 1, Cambridge, Mass., 1975).

Tacuba (A1)

See information on Azcapotzalco, which also applies to this site.

* Tenochtitlan (C4)

The remains of the recently excavated Great Temple (*Templo Mayor*), the best-known and most prominent building in the great Aztec metropolis of Tenochtitlan, can be seen adjacent to the Zocalo in downtown Mexico City.

Tenochtitlan was the Aztec capital that Cortés and his soldiers first saw in AD 1519 and conquered shortly afterwards. It was founded in AD 1325 on an island in a swampy part of Lake Texcoco in the Valley of Mexico and rapidly grew in size and importance as

150 View over the Great Temple site in modern Mexico City.

the Aztecs gained supremacy in Central Mexico. At the time of the Spanish Conquest, the city had a population that may have been in excess of 200,000 people.

Tenochtitlan was divided into four principal districts, with the major ceremonial precinct located at the center. The dominant feature of this central precinct was the huge Great Temple, a truncated pyramid surmounted by twin temples dedicated to Tlaloc (the god of rain) and Huitzilopochtli (the Aztec's patron god – the god of war). Tenochtitlan was destroyed by the Spanish conquistadors and Mexico City was built on top of its ruins. See Chapters Eight and Twelve for further details and a site plan.

Reference: Eduardo Matos Moctezuma, *The Great Temple of the Aztecs* (Thames and Hudson, London and New York, 1988).

* Teotihuacan (C4)

Located about 50 km to the northeast of Mexico City, this site is readily accessible by bus (Central Bus Station) or car, along Highway 850. It is well signposted. Facilities are available and there is a sound-and-light show in the evenings.

Teotihuacan, situated in a side valley off the east edge of the Valley of Mexico, is one of the largest sites in the Precolumbian world. It began its rise to prominence just before the time of Christ and flourished until about AD 750.

At its height Teotihuacan covered an area of about 20 sq. km, with a population of at least 120,000 and perhaps as many as 200,000 people. More than 2,000 apartment compounds have been found in recent surveys. The city was carefully laid out along a grid pattern that was oriented 15 30' east of north. There is good evidence for a degree of central planning in the city's layout and growth. Many major buildings can be found along the main north-south axis of the grid, the so-called "Street of the Dead." Among the most famous are the Pyramids of the Sun and Moon, and the Citadel, where the rulers of Teotihuacan probably lived. The city was in contact with many parts of ancient Mesoamerica and influenced a number of different regions economically and perhaps politically and religiously, as well.

Reference: Kathleen Berrin and Esther Pasztory (eds.), *Teotihuacan: Art from the City of the Gods* (Thames and Hudson, London and New York, 1993).

from Flores. Hotels and other facilities are available in Flores and Tikal. This site is best visited in the Spring.

Perhaps the largest lowland Maya site, Tikal had a population approaching 50,000 people at its height in the Late Classic Period. Long-term research by the University of Pennsylvania Museum and the Guatemalan government has revealed a sequence from about 800 BC to AD 900, when the site was largely abandoned. Tikal is particularly famous for its tall pyramid-temples, including Temples I and II which face each other across the great Central Plaza in the very heart of the urban center.

Reference: Christopher Jones, William R. Coe, and William A. Haviland, "Tikal: An Outline of its Field Study (1956–1970) and a Project Bibliography," in Victoria R. Bricker (gen. ed.) and Jeremy A. Sabloff (vol. ed.), *Supplement to the Handbook of Middle American Indians*, Vol. 1, pp. 296–312 (University of Texas Press, Austin, 1981.)

Texcoco (A2)

Texcoco is located in the Basin of Mexico and reached its height during the Late Postclassic Period. The site covered more than 4 sq. km and was probably the second largest urban center in the Basin next to Tenochtitlan. Its population has been estimated at 20,000–30,000 inhabitants. It was part of the "Triple Alliance," along with Tenochtitlan and Tlacopan, that defeated the Tepanecs in AD 1428 and paved the way for Aztec dominance of Central Mexico.

Reference: Jeffrey R. Parsons, *Prehistoric Settlement Patterns in the Texcoco Region, Mexico* (Memoirs of The Museum of Anthropology, University of Michigan, No. 3, Ann Arbor, 1971).

* Tikal (C9)

This site in the Guatemalan Lowlands can be reached by airplane from Guatemala City to the town of Flores, and then by road to Tikal (60 km from Flores). The road you should take does not have a number; follow the main highway running east from Flores and then take the side road to Tikal at El Cruce. It is possible to get a bus to the site

Tlalancaleca (C4)

Situated on the flanks of a volcano in northern Puebla. It covers some 700 hectares and flourished between 800 and 300 BC. Recent research has revealed a large number of dwellings, as well as residential and agricultural terraces. Carved stelae, large stone sarcophagi, and *talud-tablero* style architecture are all found at Tlalancaleca.

Reference: Angel Garcia Cook, "The Historical Importance of Tlaxcala in the Cultural Development of the Central Highlands," in Victoria R. Bricker (gen. ed.) and Jeremy A. Sabloff (vol. ed.), *Supplement to the Handbook of Middle American Indians*, Vol. 1, pp. 244–76 (University of Texas Press, Austin, 1981).

* Tula (C4)

Situated just outside the modern city of Tula de Allende in the state of Hidalgo, this site can easily be reached from there by car. Alternatively, tourists can travel from Mexico City along Highway 57D by car or bus (Central Bus Station), returning on the same day. The site is well signposted. Facilities are available.

Tula (or ancient Tollan) was the capital of the Toltecs. It reached its height between about AD 900 and 1100, covering an area of 14 sq. km, and had a population somewhere between 35,000 and 60,000 people. Unlike

Teotihuacan and Tenochtitlan, Tula does not show much evidence of overall city planning, although the well-known Acropolis zone of the site is an exception. The most famous of the structures in this zone is Temple B (or the Temple of Quetzalcoatl), with its huge Atlantean columns. A host of carvings found in the Acropolis emphasize the themes of death and warfare. The latter, in conjunction with legendary materials from later Aztec times, have led to the characterization of Tula and the Toltecs as militaristic and bloodthirsty. Although Tula was clearly in economic contact with many far-flung places, archaeological evidence to support the exact extent and nature of its conquests and empire remains unclear. See Chapters Seven and Twelve for further information and a site plan.

Reference: Richard A. Diehl, *Tula: The Toltec Capital of Ancient Mexico* (Thames and Hudson, London and New York, 1983).

Tzintzuntzan (C2)

Located on the shores of Lake Patzacuaro in the West Mexican state of Michoacan, Tzintzuntzan was the capital of the Tarascan region that flourished in Late Postclassic times. The Tarascans successfully repelled the military advances of the Aztecs, and they and their capital city were never brought into the Aztec empire. Tzintzuntzan is best known for a huge architectural complex at its center, featuring an immense platform crowned by five temples.

Reference: Shirley Gorenstein and Helen Perlstein Pollard, *The Tarascan Civilization: A Late Prehispanic Cultural System* (Vanderbilt University Publications in Anthropology, No. 28, Nashville, 1983).

Utatlan (E9)

Utatlan is situated in the central Guatemalan Highlands. It was the capital of the great Quiche state during Late Postclassic times until the Spanish Conquest. The full urban center lies on six adjacent plateaus and covers about 7 sq. km. Three large plazas, defined by monumental architecture, are found at Utatlan. Recent settlement research by the State University of New York-Albany indicates a regular organizational pattern throughout the city.

Reference: Robert M. Carmack, *The Quiche Mayas of Utatlan* (University of Oklahoma Press, Norman, 1981).

* Uxmal (B9)

This great Maya site has some of the most beautiful architecture anywhere in ancient Mexico. It can be reached by car or bus from Merida, capital of Yucatan, in about an hour and a half along Highway 261. The site is well signposted. There are several hotels and other facilities adjacent to the site. A sound-and-light show takes place in the evenings.

Uxmal is located in the Puuc or hilly region of the Northern Maya Lowlands and flourished in the Terminal Classic Period from about AD 800 to 1000. The city is laid out on a north-south axis, and its center contains a series of large, aesthetically beautiful structures, including the renowned Pyramid of the Magician, the Nunnery Quadrangle, and the House of the Turtles. The orientations of certain buildings, such as the imposing Palace of the Governors, appear to have had astronomical significance. Recent research indicates that the latter may have been built by "Lord Chac" as his principal residence. The architecture at Uxmal is characterized by the Puuc style of construction, featuring fine cut-stone masonry and elaborate stone mosaics with geometric and naturalistic designs on the upper façades of buildings. Uxmal is connected by a raised causeway or *sacbe* with the city of Kabah, 18 km to the southeast. Unfortunately, Uxmal has never been intensively surveyed and a full map of the city beyond its center does not exist. Thus, it is not possible to estimate its ancient population.

Reference: Alfredo Rubio Barrera, *Uxmal, Guia Oficial* (Instituto Nacional de Antropologia e Historia – Salvat Mexicana de Ediciones, Mexico, 1985).

* Xochicalco (C4)

Located nearly 40 km to the south of Cuernavaca in the state of Morelos. It is accessible by paved road just off Highway 95 or 95D, and is well signposted. No bus goes to the site itself. Facilities are available.

The site is situated to the south of the Basin of Mexico. It was an important Late

Classic-Terminal Classic center that had a brief florescence coincident with the decline of Teotihuacan. The core of Xochicalco is located on top of a terraced hill. The architecture and sculpture indicate that the site was in close contact with the Basin of Mexico, the Gulf Coast, and the Maya Lowlands. Most of the population lived on residential terraces that line the sides of the hills surrounding the civic core.

Reference: Kenneth Hirth, "Roads, Thoroughfares, and Avenues of Power at Xochicalco, Mexico," in Charles D. Trombold (ed.), *Ancient Road Networks and Settlement Hierarchies in the New World*, pp. 211–221 (Cambridge University Press, Cambridge, 1991).

Xochimilco (B1)

See information on Azcapotzalco, which also applies to this site.

Yaxchilan (D8)

Yaxchilan is a major Classic Maya site located on a bluff overlooking the western bank of the Usumacinta River in the Southern Lowlands. It is renowned for its well-preserved Late Classic stone sculpture including monuments and lintels over the doorways of elite buildings. Recent research on the hieroglyphic inscriptions at the site have revealed a dynastic sequence, while other studies have related Yaxchilan to nearby sites, including Bonampak and Piedras Negras.

Reference: Carolyn Elaine Tate, *Yaxchilan: The Design of a Maya Ceremonial City* (University of Texas Press, Austin, 1992).

Yucuita (D5)

Yucuita was the earliest Mixtec urban center. It is a complex site located in the Nochixtlan Valley of Oaxaca. Research by Vanderbilt University indicates that the site flourished between 200 BC and AD 300. It covers about 2 sq. km and has several hundred structures within its center. Yucuita was the political and economic capital of the Valley during this part of the Late Preclassic Period and may have had a population of 8,000 inhabitants.

Reference: Ronald Spores, "Ramos Phase Urbanization in the Mixteca Alta," in Kent Flannery and Joyce Marcus (eds) *The Cloud People*, pp. 120–23 (Academic Press, New York, 1983).

Yucunudahui (D5)

Situated along an L-shaped ridgetop in the Nochixtlan Valley of Oaxaca. One arm of the site is approximately 3 km long, while the other is 1 km with a width of about 250 m. Residential terraces are located below the ridgetop, while the ceremonial locus, including a ball court, is on top. Recent research by Vanderbilt University has shown that the site dates principally to the Classic Period, especially to Late Classic times.

Reference: Ronald Spores, "Yucunudahui," in Kent Flannery and Joyce Marcus (eds) *The Cloud People*, p. 155–58 (Academic Press, New York, 1983).

Zaculeu (D8)

Located in the western Guatemalan Highlands near the modern city of Huehuetenango. A large urban core was built up over a long period of time, from the Early Classic through the Late Postclassic Period. The site was the capital of the Maya people who were known as the Mam. During the Late Postclassic, Zaculeu and the Mam came under the control of the Quiche whose influence is reflected in some buildings of that time. The residential area of the site is reported to have been large but has never been intensively investigated.

Reference: Richard B. Woodbury and Aubrey S. Trik, *The Ruins of Zaculeu, Guatemala* (United Fruit Company, Richmond, Virginia, 1955).

Zempoala (C5)

Zempoala (or Cempoala) is located on the Gulf Coast of Veracruz. This large city flourished throughout the Postclassic Period. It is at this site that Cortés landed to begin his march to Tenochtitlan. Zempoala was surrounded by a wall and had a large ceremonial complex, including five pyramids with temples, and a round temple. Parts of aqueducts which supplied the city with fresh water have been found.

Reference: José García Payon, "Archaeology of Central Veracruz," in Robert Wauchope (gen. ed.) and Gordon F. Ekholm and Ignacio Bernal (vol. eds), *Handbook of Middle American Indians*, Vol. 11, pp. 505–542 (University of Texas Press, Austin, 1971).

Further reading

My knowledge and understanding of ancient Mexico has been built up over the years through first-hand experience in the field, innumerable discussions with colleagues, and the reading of at least a goodly portion of the huge literature that archaeologists, ethnohistorians, ethnographers, and other scholars have produced. In the pages below, I cite a very small part of this literature that I think will be of use to readers who wish to follow up some of the specific topics discussed in the text.

General overview

For overviews of ancient Mexico as a whole, combining Michael Coe's two Ancient Peoples and Places books, *Mexico* (Fourth edition, Thames and Hudson, London and New York, 1994) and *The Maya* (Fifth edition, Thames and Hudson, London and New York, 1993), provides a good, broad introduction to the subject. Students looking for more detailed texts would do well to consult either Richard E.W. Adams' *Prehistoric Mesoamerica* (Revised edition, University of Oklahoma Press, 1991) or Muriel Porter Weaver's *The Aztecs, Maya, and their Predecessors* (Third edition, Academic Press, New York, 1993). Another stimulating book with a broad perspective is Richard Blanton *et al.*, *Ancient Mesoamerica* (Second edition, Cambridge University Press, Cambridge and New York, 1993). A very useful general introduction to the art of Mesoamerica is Mary Ellen Miller's book *The Art of Mesoamerica* (Second edition, Thames and Hudson, London and New York, 1996). See also George Kubler, *Art and Architecture of Ancient America*, (Second and third editions, Harmondsworth and Baltimore (Pelican), 1975 and 1984).

An introduction to pre-industrial urbanism can be found in Kingsley Davis (editor) *Cities: Their Origins, Growth and Human Impact; Readings from Scientific American* (W.H. Freeman, San Francisco, 1973); also see Lewis Mumford, *The City in History* (Harcourt, Brace, and World, New York, 1961), and Mason Hammond, *The City in the Ancient World* (Harvard University Press, Cambridge, 1972). Chapter Seven ("The Origins of Urban Society: In Search of Utopia") of Charles Redman's *The Rise of Civilization: From Early Farmers to Urban Society in the Ancient Near East* (W.H. Freeman, San Francisco, 1978) offers a very useful review of various archaeological definitions of cities and the varied theoretical approaches scholars have employed to study them. A comprehensive up-to-date overview of the development of cities and complex societies is contained in Anthony Andrews, *First Cities* (St. Remy Press and Smithsonian Institution Books, Montreal and Washington D.C., 1995); see also Henry Wright's superb article "The Evolution of Civilization" in *American Archaeology: Past and Future*, edited by David Meltzer, Don Fowler, and Jeremy Sabloff (Smithsonian Institution Press, Washington, D.C., 1986).

San Lorenzo

The principal source on San Lorenzo is the two-volume site report by Michael Coe and Richard Diehl, *In the Land of the Olmec* (University of Texas Press, Austin, 1980). A useful summary of this research can be found in Michael Coe, "San Lorenzo Tenochtitlan," in *Supplement to the Handbook of Middle American Indians*, Vol. 1, Victoria Bricker (general editor) and Jeremy Sabloff (volume editor) (University of Texas Press, Austin, 1981). Other introductions to the Olmec include Elizabeth Benson (editor) *Dumbarton Oaks Conference on the Olmecs* (Dumbarton Oaks, Washington D.C., 1968), Ignacio Bernal, *The Olmec World* (University of California Press, Berkeley, 1969), and Michael Coe, *America's First Civilization* (American Heritage, New York, 1968). More recent views can be found in Robert Sharer and David Grove (editors), *Regional Perspectives on the Olmec* (Cambridge University Press, Cambridge, 1989). A fine discussion of a contemporaneous site outside the Gulf Coast Lowlands in presented in David Grove's *Chalcatzingo* (Thames and Hudson, London and New York, 1984). The innovative study of modern agriculture in the Gulf Coast area is Thomas Killion, *Agriculture and Residential Site Structure among Campesinos in Southern Veracruz, Mexico: A Foundation for Archaeological Inference*, Ph.D. dissertation, University of New Mexico (University Microfilms, Ann Arbor, 1987); also see Thomas Killion (editor) *Gardens of Prehistory: The Archaeology of Settlement Agriculture in Greater Mesoamerica* (University of Alabama Press, Tuscaloosa, 1992).

A helpful introduction to the question of transoceanic contacts can be found in *Man Across the Sea*, edited by Carroll Riley, J. Charles Kelley, Campbell Pennington, and Robert Rands (University of Texas Press, Austin, 1971); also see my introductory essay in *Archaeology: Myth and Reality; Readings from Scientific American* (W.H. Freeman, San Francisco, 1982). Contrasting arguments, pro and con, regarding the presence of transoceanic influence on New World cultures are well presented in (pro) Stephen Jett, "Precolumbian Transoceanic Contacts," in *Ancient South Americans*, edited by Jesse Jennings (W.H. Freeman, San Francisco, 1983) and (con) Philip Phillips, "The Role of Transpacific Contacts in the Development of New World Pre-Columbian Civilizations," in the *Handbook of Middle American Indians*, Vol. 4, edited by Robert Wauchope (general editor) and Gordon Willey and Gordon Ekholm (volume editors) (University of Texas Press, Austin, 1966). Specifically in relation to ancient Mexico, a good start for understanding the pro-diffusion point of view would be Betty Meggers, "The Transpacific Origin of Mesoamerican Civilization: A Preliminary View of the Evidence and its Theoretical Implications," *American Anthropologist*, Vol. 77, No. 1 (1975): 1–27; also see Ivan Van Sertima, *They Came Before Columbus* (Random House, New York, 1976) and R.A. Jairazbhoy, *Ancient Egyptians and Chinese in America* (Rowman and Littlefield, Totowa, New Jersey, 1974). Finally, Robert Wauchope's *Lost Tribes and Sunken Continents* (University of Chicago Press, Chicago, 1962) still remains the best general introduction to the question of pseudoscientific views of long-distance diffusion, while Stephen Williams, *Fantastic Archaeology* (University of Pennsylvania Press, Philadelphia, 1991) is an excellent overview of pseudoarchaeology in general.

Monte Alban

The best introduction to recent research in the Valley of Oaxaca is Joyce Marcus and Kent Flannery, *Zapotec Civilization* (Thames and Hudson, London and New York, 1996). Settlement research at Monte Alban is summarized in Richard Blanton's *Monte Alban: Settlement Patterns at the Ancient Zapotec Capital* (Academic Press, New York, 1978); also see two articles in the *Supplement to the Handbook of Middle American Indians*, Vol. 1, Victoria Bricker (general editor) and Jeremy Sabloff (volume editor) (University of Texas Press, Austin, 1981): Richard Blanton and Stephen Kowalewski, "Monte Alban and After in the Valley of Oaxaca," and Richard Blanton, "The Rise of Cities." Another article in the *Supplement*, "The Preceramic and Formative in the Valley of Oaxaca" by Kent Flannery, Joyce Marcus, and Stephen Kowalewski, provides useful background to the rise of Monte Alban. For information about astronomical interpretations at Monte Alban, the best place to begin is Anthony Aveni's *Skywatchers of Ancient Mexico* (University of Texas Press, Austin, 1980); also see the recent article by Damon Peeler and Marcus Winter on "Building J at Monte Alban: A Correction and Reassessment of the Astronomical Hypothesis," *Latin American Antiquity*, Vol. 6, No. 4 (1995): 362–9. Other discussions can be found in Anthony Aveni and Robert Linsley, "Mound J, Monte Alban: Possible Astronomical Orientation," *American Antiquity*, Vol. 37, No. 4 (1972): 528–31; Anthony Aveni, "Concepts of Positional Astronomy Employed in Ancient Mesoamerican Architecture," in *Native American Astronomy*, edited by Aveni (University of Texas Press, Austin, 1977); and Anthony Aveni, "Astronomy in Ancient Mesoamerica," in *In Search of Ancient Astronomies*, edited by E.C. Krupp (McGraw-Hill, New York, 1978). See also Anthony Aveni, *Ancient Astronomers* (St. Remy Press and Smithsonian Institution Books, Montreal and Washington D.C., 1993). For discussions of possible functions of Building J, see Joyce Marcus, "Zapotec Writing," *Scientific American*, Vol. 242, No. 2 (1980): 50–64; and "The Conquest Slabs of Building J, Monte Alban," in *The Cloud People*, edited by Kent Flannery and Joyce Marcus (Academic Press, New York, 1983). A good overview of the growth of complexity in Oaxaca, and particularly at San Jose Mogote, can be found in Joyce Marcus's "Zapotec Chiefdoms and the Nature of Formative Religions," in *Regional Perspectives on the Olmec*, edited by Robert Sharer and David Grove (Cambridge University Press, Cambridge, 1989); see also Kent Flannery and Joyce Marcus, *Early Formative Pottery of the Valley of Oaxaca, Mexico* (Museum of Anthropology, University of Michigan, Ann Arbor, 1994).

Maya

Fortunately, a number of good, up-to-date texts on the ancient Maya are available, although the rapidly changing nature of Maya studies may soon make them dated. A number of different books with varying coverage and perspectives can be recommended including Michael Coe, *The Maya* (Fifth edition, Thames and Hudson, London and New York, 1993); T. Patrick Culbert, *Maya Civilization* (St.

Remy Press and Smithsonian Institution Books, Montreal and Washington D.C., 1993); Robert Sharer, *The Ancient Maya* (Fifth edition, Stanford University Press, Stanford, 1994); and Gene Stuart and George Stuart, *The Lost Kingdoms of the Maya* (National Geographic Society, Washington, D.C., 1993). See also my book *The New Archaeology and the Ancient Maya* (W. H. Freeman, New York, 1994). A fine introduction to Maya architectural and site planning is George Andrews' *Maya Cities: Placemaking and Urbanization* (University of Oklahoma Press, Norman, 1975), while Linda Schele and Mary Miller, *The Blood of Kings* (Kimbell Art Museum, Fort Worth, 1986), Linda Schele and David Freidel, *A Forest of Kings* (Morrow, New York, 1990), T. P. Culbert (editor) *Classic Maya Political History* (Cambridge University Press, Cambridge, 1991), and Michael Coe, *Breaking the Maya Code* (Thames and Hudson, London and New York, 1992) provide excellent overviews of some of the new advances in the study of Maya hieroglyphs. The function of "palaces" is carefully examined by Peter Harrison in *The Central Acropolis, Tikal, Guatemala: A Preliminary Study of the Functions of its Structural Components during the Late Classic Period*, Ph.D. dissertation, University of Pennsylvania (University Microfilms, Ann Arbor, 1970). Recent research on the Terminal Classic drought is discussed in D. Hodell *et al.*, *Nature*, Vol. 375 (1995): 391–4, 1995.

Cerros: The results of the research at the site by Southern Methodist University is available in a variety of publications. The most useful introduction to this work can be found in *Archaeology at Cerros, Belize, Central America, Volume I: An Interim Report* (Southern Methodist University Press, Dallas, 1986), edited by Robin Robertson and David Freidel; also see "The Maya City of Cerros" by David Freidel, Robin Robertson, and Maynard Cliff in *Archaeology*, Vol. 35, No. 4 (1982): 12–22. David Freidel's "Culture Areas and Interaction Spheres: Contrasting Approaches to the Emergence of Civilization in the Maya Lowlands," *American Antiquity*, Vol. 44, No. 1 (1979): 36–56, looks at Cerros in a wider perspective.

Palenque: There is no one, good overall study of Palenque available. However, Alberto Ruz, who discovered the great tomb beneath the Temple of the Inscriptions, wrote a series of reports on his excavations at Palenque for the *Anales* of the Instituto Nacional de Antropologia e Historia of Mexico (between 1952 and 1962). The INAH guidebook to Palenque also serves as a good, brief introduction to the site. Other publications of interest include Peter Matthews and Linda Schele's path-breaking, "Lords of Palenque – The Glyphic Evidence," in *Primera Mesa Redonda de Palenque*, edited by Merle Greene Robertson (Robert Louis Stevenson School, Pebble Beach, 1974); Alberto Ruz, "Gerontocracy at Palenque," in *Social Process in Maya Prehistory*, edited by Norman Hammond (Academic Press, London and New York, 1977); Norman Hammond and Theya Molleson, "Huguenot Weavers and Kings: Anthropological Assessment Versus Documentary Record of Age at Death," *Mexicon*, Vol. 16, No. 4 (1995): 75–7; Merle Greene Robertson's beautifully illustrated, on-going, multi-volume, *The Sculpture of Palenque* (Princeton University Press, Princeton, 1983–); and Beatriz de la Fuente, *La Escultura de Palenque*, Estudios y Fuentes del

Arte en Mexico, XX (Instituto de Investigaciones Esteticas, UNAM, Mexico, D.F., 1965). Linda Schele's "Architectural Development and Political History at Palenque" in *City-States of the Maya: Art and Architecture*, edited by Elizabeth Benson (Rocky Mountain Institute for Pre-Columbian Studies, Denver, 1986) is an important and useful contribution, as is Floyd Lounsbury's "Recent Work in the Decipherment of Palenque's Hieroglyphic Inscriptions," *Am. Anthro.* Vol. 93 (1991): 809–25.

Uxmal: There has never been a full-scale study of Uxmal and, to date, no published map of the overall settlement exists (alas, the same is true for Palenque). A good introduction to Uxmal, including a map of the site core, can be found in Harry Pollock's exhaustive survey, *The Puuc, An Architectural Survey of the Hill Country of Yucatan and Northern Campeche, Mexico*, Memoirs of the Peabody Museum, Harvard University, Vol. 19 (Cambridge, 1980). Settlement research at the site is discussed in Alfredo Barrera Rubio's "Patron de asentamiento en el area de Uxmal, Yucatan," *XVI Mesa Redonda de la Sociedad Mexicana de Antropologia*, Vol. II (Saltillo, Mexico, 1980). Research on the inscriptions of the palace of the Governors is summarized in Jeff Karl Kowalski's "Lords of the Northern Maya," *Expedition*, Vol. 27, No. 3 (1985): 50–60; also see his *The House of the Governor; A Maya Palace at Uxmal, Yucatan, Mexico* (University of Oklahoma Press, Norman, 1987).

A useful introduction to the ancient Maya ball game is Christopher Jones' "The Rubber Ball Game," *Expedition*, Vol. 27, No. 2 (1985): 44–52. New, provocative views on the game are contained in Linda Schele and Mary Ellen Miller, *The Blood of Kings* (Kimbell Art Museum, Fort Worth, 1986), and in Robert Santley, Michael Berman, and Rani Alexander, "The Politicalization of the Mesoamerican Ball Game and Its Implications for the Interpretation of the Distribution of Ball Courts in Central Mexico," in *The Native American Ball Game*, edited by Vernon Scarborough and David Wilcox (University of Arizona Press, Tucson, 1991).

Teotihuacan

The best brief introduction to Teotihuacan in Rene Millon's article, "Teotihuacan: City, State, and Civilization," in the *Supplement to the Handbook of Middle American Indians*, Vol. 1, Victoria Bricker (general editor) and Jeremy Sabloff (volume editor) (University of Texas Press, Austin, 1981). The reader can then follow up the article by examining the detailed map of the city that Millon, Bruce Drewiit, and George Cowgill published in *The Teotihuacan Map* (University of Texas Press, Austin, 1973). A general overview can be found in Eduardo Matos, *Teotihuacan: City of Gods* (Rizzoloi, New York, 1990). Reports on some of the recent research at the ancient city are found in *Teotihuacan 1980–1982: Neuvas Interpretaciones*, edited by Ruben Cabrera, Ignacio Rodriguez, and Noel Morelos (INAH, Mexico, D.F., 1991); Evelyn Rattray, *The Oaxaca Barrio at Teotihuacàn* (University of the Americas, Puebla, 1993); Suburo Sùgiyama, "Worldview Materialized in Teotihuacan, Mexico," in *Latin American Antiquity*, Vol. 4, No. 2 (1993): 103–29; and *Life and Death in the Ancient City of Teotihuacan: A Modern Paleodemographic Analysis* by Rebecca Storey (University of Alabama Press, Tuscaloosa, 1992); see also *Art, Ideology, and the City of Teotihuacan*, edited by Janet Berlo (Dumbarton Oaks, Washington D.C., 1992) and *Teotihuacan: Art from the City of the Gods*, edited by Kathleen Berrin and Esther Pasztory (Thames and Hudson, London and New York, 1993). Two informative articles are Michael Spence, "Craft Production and Polity in Early Teotihuacan," in *Trade and Exchange in Early Mesoamerica*, edited by Kenneth Hirth (University of New Mexico Press, Albuquerque, 1984); and George Cowgill, Jeffrey Altschul, and Rebecca Sload, "Spatial Analysis of Teotihuacan: A Mesoamerican Metropolis," in *Intrasite Spatial Analysis in Archaeology*, edited by Harold Hietala (Cambridge University Press, Cambridge, 1984). The paintings of Teotihuacan are analyzed in Arthur Miller's *Mural Painting of Teotihuacan* (Dumbarton Oaks, Washington, D.C., 1973). The place of Teotihuacan in the settlement history of the Valley of Mexico as a whole is discussed in *The Valley of Mexico*, edited by Eric Wolf (University of New Mexico Press, Albuquerque, 1976), and in *The Basin of Mexico* by William Sanders, Jeffrey Parsons, and Robert Santley (Academic Press, New York, 1979). The growth of complexity in Central Mexico in relation to trade and transportation costs is ably discussed by Robert Drennan in "Long Distance Movement of Goods in the Mesoamerican Formative and Classic," *American Antiquity*, Vol. 49, No. 1 (1984): 27–43. The study of contemporary ceramic manufacture mentioned in the discussion of Teotihuacan is Philip Arnold's *Domestic Ceramic Production and Spatial Organization: A Mexican Case Study in Ethnoarchaeology* (Cambridge University Press, Cambridge, 1991).

Tula

The best general introduction to the site is Richard Diehl's *Tula, the Toltec Capital of Ancient Mexico* (Thames and Hudson, London and New York, 1983). See also Dan Healan, *Tula of the Toltecs* (University of Iowa Press, Iowa City, 1989). The period just before the rise of Tula is discussed in *Mesoamerica After the Decline of Teotihuacan, AD 700–900*, Janet Berlo and Richard Diehl (editors) (Dumbarton Oaks, Washington, D.C., 1989). For a broad overview of the the Toltecs, see Nigel Davies, *The Toltecs Until the Fall of Tula* (University of Oklahoma Press, Norman 1977). More technical information can be found in *Studies of Ancient Tollan: A Report of the University of Missouri-Columbia Tula Archaeological Project*, edited by Richard Diehl, University of Missouri Monographs in Anthropology, No. 1 (Columbia, 1974); *Proyecto Tula, Primera y Segunda Partes*, edited by Eduardo Matos Moctezuma (Departmento de Monumentos Prehispanicos, INAH, 1974–1976); and Alba Guadalupe Mastache, Ana Maria Crespo, Robert Cobean, and Dan Healan, *Estudios sobre la antigua ciudad de Tula* (Departmento de Monumentos Prehispanicos, INAH, 1982). The manufacture of stone bowls is discussed by Noemi Castillo Tejera, "Technologia de una vasija en travertino," *Boletin del Instituto Nacional de Antropologia e Historia*, No. 41, 1970.

Tenochtitlan

The subject of the Aztecs is well covered in a number of useful introductory volumes including Frances Berdan,

The Aztecs of Central Mexico: An Imperial Society (Holt, Rinehart, and Winston, New York, 1982); Elizabeth Boone, *The Aztec World* (St. Remy Press and Smithsonian Institution Books, Montreal and Washington D.C., 1994); Warwick Bray, *The Everyday Life of the Aztecs* (Batsford, London, and G.P. Putnam's Sons, New York,1968); Inga Clendinnen, *Aztecs* (Cambridge University Press, Cambridge, 1991); Nigel Davies, *The Aztecs: A History* (MacMillan, London, 1973 [republished by the University of Oklahoma Press, Norman, 1980]); Brian Fagan, *The Aztecs* (W.H. Freeman, New York, 1984); Jacques Soustelle, *Daily Life of the Aztecs on the Eve of the Spanish Conquest* (MacMillan, New York, 1962 [republished by Stanford University Press, Stanford, 1970]); Gene Stuart, *The Mighty Aztecs* (National Geographic Society, Washington, D.C., 1981); and Richard Townsend *The Aztecs* (Thames and Hudson, London and New York, 1992). An excellent introduction to the new discoveries at the Templo Mayor can be found in Eduardo Matos Moctezuma's *The Great Temple of the Aztecs* (Thames and Hudson, London and New York, 1988); also see *The Aztec Templo Mayor*, edited by Elizabeth Boone (Dumbarton Oaks, Washington, D.C., 1987). The subject of chinampas is covered by Michael Coe in "The Chinampas of Mexico," *Scientific American*, July, 1964; also see Edward Calnek, "Settlement Pattern and Chinampa Agriculture at Tenochtitlan," *American Antiquity*, Vol. 37, No. 1 (1972). Another useful article by Calnek is "The Internal Structure of Tenochtitlan" in *The Valley of Mexico*, edited by Eric Wolf (University of New Mexico Press, Albuquerque, 1976). Readers might also wish to consult Charles Gibson, *The Aztecs Under Spanish Rule: A History of the Indians of the Valley of Mexico, 1519–1810* (Stanford University Press, Stanford, 1964); Ross Hassig, *Trade, Tribute, and Transportation: The Sixteenth-Century Political Economy of the Valley of Mexico* (University of Oklahoma Press, Norman, 1985); and Rudolph van Zantwijk, *The Aztec Arrangement: The Social History of Pre-Spanish Mexico* (University of Oklahoma Press, Norman, 1985). The writings of Fray Bernardino de Sahagun have been expertly translated by Arthur Anderson and Charles Dibble in the multivolume *Florentine Codex: General History of the Things of New Spain* (University of Utah Press and the School of American Research, Salt Lake City and Santa Fe, 1950–1969). There has been a recent surge in archaeological studies of the Aztecs. Some of this new research on the Aztecs is discussed in Mary Hodge and Michael Smith (editors) *Economies and Polities in the Aztec Realm* (Institute for Mesoamerican Studies, Albany, 1994).

Methodology

Fortunately, there are a number of good introductory textbooks providing overviews of current thought on archaeological method and theory that are comprehensible to general readers. Among the most recent texts, Colin Renfrew and Paul Bahn, *Archaeology: Theories, Methods, and Practice* (Second edition, Thames and Hudson, London and New York, 1996); Brian Hayden, *Archaeology: The Science of Once and Future Things* (W. H. Freeman, New York, 1993); Brian Fagan, *In the Beginning, An Introduction to Archaeology*, (Seventh edition, HarperCollins, New York, 1991); Robert Sharer and Wendy Ashmore, *Archaeo-

logy, Discovering Our Past* (Second edition, Mayfield, Mountain View, 1993); and David Thomas, *Archaeology: Down to Earth* (Harcourt, Brace, Jovanovich, Fort Worth, 1991) can all be recommended.

With regards to archaeological method, in general, and analogical reasoning, in particular, the most innovative and influential thinker in the field has been Lewis Binford. His most accessible overview of method and theory can be found in *In Pursuit of the Past* (Thames and Hudson, London and New York, 1983); see also Gordon Willey and Jeremy Sabloff *A History of American Archaeology* (Third edition, W. H. Freeman, New York, 1993), especially Chapters 6–8. A fine case example of the building of bridging theory can be found in Robin Torrence's *Production and Exchange of Stone Tools* (Cambridge University Press, Cambridge, 1986). For a general discussion on the formation of the archaeological record, see Michael Schiffer, *Formation Processes of the Archaeological Record* (University of New Mexico Press, Albuquerque, 1987). Recent debates are clearly discussed in Robert Preucel (editor) *Processual and Postprocessual Archaeologies: Multiple Ways of Knowing the Past* (Center for Archaeological Investigations, Carbondale, 1991).

A provocative discussion of the use of analogy in archaeological reasoning can be found in Richard Gould and Patty Jo Watson, "A Dialogue on the Meaning and Use of Analogy in Ethnoarchaeological Reasoning," *Journal of Anthropological Archaeology*, Vol. 1 (1982): 355–81; also see Patty Jo Watson, Steven LeBlanc, and Charles Redman, *Archaeological Explanation; The Scientific Method of Archaeology* (Columbia University Press, New York, 1984). Alison Wylie's "The Reaction Against Analogy," in *Advances in Archaeological Method and Theory*, Vol. 8, edited by Michael Schiffer (Academic Press, New York, 1985) offers very useful insights into archaeological thinking on analogy.

Good introductions to ethnoarchaeology can be found in Richard Gould (editor) *Explorations in Ethnoarchaeology* (University of New Mexico Press, Albuquerque, 1978); Carol Kramer (editor) *Ethnoarchaeology* (Columbia University Press, New York, 1979); Richard Gould, *Living Archaeology* (Cambridge University Press, Cambridge, 1980), and William Longacre and James Skibo (editors) *Kalinga Ethnoarchaeology: Expanding Archaeological Method and Theory* (Smithsonian Institution Press, Washington D.C., 1994). Ivor Noël Hume, *Historical Archaeology* (Knopf, New York, 1969); Stanley South, *Method and Theory in Historical Archaeology* (Academic Press, New York, 1977); and Mark Leone and Potter Parker, *The Recovery of Meaning: Historical Archaeology in the Eastern United States* (Smithsonian Institution Press, Washington D.C., 1988) are good places to begin an examination of this subject.

For further discussions of the use of analogies and historic data in the Maya area see Evon Z. Vogt, "The Genetic Model and Maya Cultural Development," in *Desarrollo Cultural de Los Mayas*, edited by Evon Vogt and Alberto Ruz (Universidad Nacional Autonoma de Mexico, Mexico D.F., 1964) and "On the Application of the Phylogenetic Model to the Maya," in *North American Indian Anthropology*, edited by Raymond DeMallie and Alfonso Ortiz (University of Oklahoma Press, Norman,

1994). Also see Elizabeth Graham, Grant Jones, and Robert Kautz, "Archaeology and Ethnohistory on a Spanish Colonial Frontier: An Interim Report on the Macal-Tipu Project in Western Belize," in *The Lowland Maya Postclassic*, edited by Arlen Chase and Prudence Rice (University of Texas Press, Austin, 1985) and David Freidel and Jeremy Sabloff, *Cozumel: Late Maya Settlement Patterns* (Academic Press, New York, 1984). Two articles of mine might be of additional interest: "Classic Maya Settlement Pattern Studies: Past Problems, Future Prospects," in Evon Vogt and Richard Leventhal (editors) *Prehistoric Settlement Pattern Studies: Retrospect and Prospect* (University of New Mexico Press, Albuquerque, 1983); and "Interaction Among Classic Maya Polities: A Preliminary Examination," in Colin Renfrew and John Cherry (editors) *Peer Polity Interaction and Socio-Political Change* (Cambridge University Press, Cambridge, 1986). Finally, for a general example of how history, archaeology, an ethnology can productively be combined, the reader might wish to look at Nancy Farriss' fine *Maya Society Under Colonial Rule* (Princeton University Press, Princeton, 1984).

Notes to the text

1 Bernal Díaz, *The Conquest of New Spain*, translated by J.M. Cohen (Penguin, Harmondsworth, 1963), p. 228.

2 *Ibid.*, p. 234.

3 Lewis Mumford, *The City in History: Its Origins, Its Transformations, Its Prospects* (Harcourt, Brace, Jovanovich, New York, 1961), p. 3.

4 Charles L. Redman, *The Rise of Civilization: From Early Farmers to Urban Society in the Ancient Near East* (W.H. Freeman, San Francisco, 1978), p. 216.

5 Kingsley Davis, "Introduction" in *Cities: Their Origins, Growth, and Human Impact; Readings from Scientific American* (W.H. Freeman, San Francisco, 1973), p. 1.

6 I have not used names for the individuals in this vignette and the ones to follow. Except for the Aztecs, we do not really know what the everyday names of the non-elite ancient peoples discussed here were. It might be possible to reconstruct such names on the basis of information from historic sources but I have not attempted this because there is significant scholarly controversy about what language some of the peoples of Precolumbian Mexico spoke. For example, there are arguments about what the language of the Olmecs was, while scholars also disagree about what the ancient Teotihuacanos spoke.

7 René Millon "Teotihuacan: City, State, and Civilization," in *Supplement to the Handbook of Middle American Indians*, Vol. 1, Victoria Bricker (General Editor) and Jeremy Sabloff (Volume Editor) (University of Texas Press, Austin 1981), p. 212.

8 *Ibid.*, p. 236.

9 George Andrews, *Maya Cities: Placemaking and Urbanization* (University of Oklahoma Press, Norman, 1975), p. 295.

10 Bernal Díaz, *The Conquest of New Spain*, translated by J.M. Cohen (Penguin, Harmondsworth, 1963), p. 216.

11 Hernan Cortés, *Letter from Mexico*, translated and edited by A.R. Pagden (Grossman, New York, 1971), p. 102.

12 Recent research suggests that the Aztecs may have settled in Central Mexico earlier than previously thought, as reported by J. Parsons, E. Brumfiel, and M. Hodge at the 1995 meeting of the Society for American Archaeology: J. Marcus pers. comm.

13 Michael Coe, "The Chinampas of Mexico," *Scientific American*, July 1964 (reprinted in *Pre-Columbian Archaeology; Readings from Scientific American*, edited by Gordon Willey and Jeremy Sabloff (W.H. Freeman, San Francisco, 1980), p. 127).

14 David Grove, *Chalcatzingo* (Thames and Hudson, London and New York, 1984), p. 129.

15 *Ibid.*, p. 155.

16 Kent Flannery, "The Cultural Evolution of Civilizations," *Annual Review of Ecology and Systematics*, Vol. 3, 1972, p. 409.

17 *Ibid.*

18 Henry Wright, "The Evolution of Civilizations," in *American Archaeology: Past and Future*, edited by David Meltzer, Don Fowler, and Jeremy A. Sabloff, pp. 323–365 (Smithsonian Institution Press, Washington, D.C., 1986).

List of illustrations

List of illustrations

126 "Conquest slab" from Structure J, Monte Alban. Photo courtesy Joyce Marcus.
127 Structure J, Monte Alban. Photo author.
128 Isometric view of Teotihuacan. After G. Kubler.
129 General map of central area of Teotihuacan. After R. Millon, "Teotihuacan," *Scientific American* (1967):5.
130 Modern ceramic manufacture in the Tuxtlas region, Mexico. Photo courtesy Philip Arnold.
131 Plan of Cerros. After Robertson and Freidel, 1986.
132 Wall painting from the Temple of the Warriors, Chichen Itza. After *The Art of the Maya*, Carnegie Institution of Washington.
133 Aerial view of Cerros, showing canal. Photo courtesy David Freidel.
134 Plan, Palenque. Drawing ML Design after Henri Stierlin, *Living*

Architecture: Mayan (Fribourg, 1964).
135 Temple of the Inscriptions at Palenque. After Stierlin, 1964 (see above).
136 Temple of the Inscriptions, Palenque. Photo author.
137 Plan, Uxmal. Drawing ML Design after Stierlin, 1964 (see above).
138 Great ball court relief. After Marquina, 1951 (see above).
139 *Palma*, H 58cm (22⅞in). Museo Nacional de Antropología, Mexico. Photo Irmgard Groth-Kimball.
140 Ballcourt marker, H 213cm (84in). Museo Nacional de Antropología, Mexico. Photo Mary Ellen Miller.
141 Stone yoke, H 45.5cm (18in). Photo courtesy American Museum of Natural History, New York.
142 Tula Grande ground plan. Courtesy R. Diehl.

143 Reconstruction drawing of the Canal Locality, Tula. Courtesy Dan M. Healan (see *World Archaeology*, Vol. 9, No. 2 (1977): 140–156).
144 Plan of the excavated remains of the Great Temple. After Matos, 1988.
145 Eagle Warrior, H 168 cm (66 in). Instituto Nacional de Antropología, e Historia, Mexico. Photo Mary Ellen Miller.
146 Chamber III, Tenochtitlan. Courtesy the Great Temple Project, Mexico City.
147 Map of Mesoamerica. Drawing Hanni Bailey.
148 Ball court, Chichen Itza. Photo Macduff Everton.
149 View from the North Group of temples, Palenque. Photo Macduff Everton.
150 View of Great Temple site, Mexico City. Photo Macduff Everton.

Acknowledgments

Discussions with many scholars, too numerous to mention, have sharpened and improved my thinking about the Precolumbian world. I am particularly indebted to my helpful and stimulating colleagues and students at the University of Pittsburgh and the University of New Mexico. The academic year (1984–1985) I spent as Overseas Visiting Fellow at St John's College, Cambridge, England, while on sabbatical leave from the University of New Mexico, enabled me to get a good start on this book. Many colleagues in Cambridge, at both St John's and the Department of Archaeology, helped make that year very educational and productive. I especially wish to thank the late Glyn Daniel, who was so supportive in the early stages of writing, and whom I will deeply miss. I am also indebted to Ruth Daniel, Ben Farmer, John Coles, John Alexander, Ian Hodder, Paul Mellars, Catherine Hills, Olivier de Montmollin, Norman Hammond, Jean Wilson, and the Master and Fellows of St John's College for their generosity and friendship. I would particularly like to single out Colin and Jane Renfrew who did so much to make the year an unforgettable one. They have my deepest gratitude.

My ideas about the archaeological world in general have been honed through innumerable conversations with Lew Binford, while much of my understanding of ancient civilizations has been broadened and strengthened by discussions with Gordon Willey for more than twenty years. I am indebted to both of them.

The seed of the idea for this book was first planted unknowingly by John Noble Wilford of *The New York Times* whose stimulating questions during a visit to the site of Sayil starting me thinking about how to answer questions I am frequently asked by students and educated laypeople. I thank him for this stimulus.

The valuable comments of Dick Drennan, Brian Fagan, Gordon Willey, Merrilee Salmon, and an anonymous reviewer on an earlier draft of the book were of much aid to me, and where I ignored their suggestions it was clearly at my own risk. Joyce Marcus kindly made some unpublished material available to me, and I also wish to thank and acknowledge my colleagues who supplied illustrative materials. I am grateful, too, to Macduff Everton whose beautiful and innovative photographs clearly enhance the book. And, finally, I wish to thank Thames and Hudson, which, from my perspective, has a deserved reputation for being a superb publisher with which to work.

In the preparation of this updated edition, I particularly wish to thank Joyce Marcus for her many helpful suggestions.

This book is dedicated to Paula Lynne Weinberg Sabloff, my wife, for her love and confidence in me. I am deeply appreciative of the innumerable hours she spent many years ago, teaching me how to write clearly. Any merit that this work might have is in no small part due to her unstinting support.

Index

Numbers in *italic* refer to illustrations
Reference points after site names refer to the map on pages 200–201